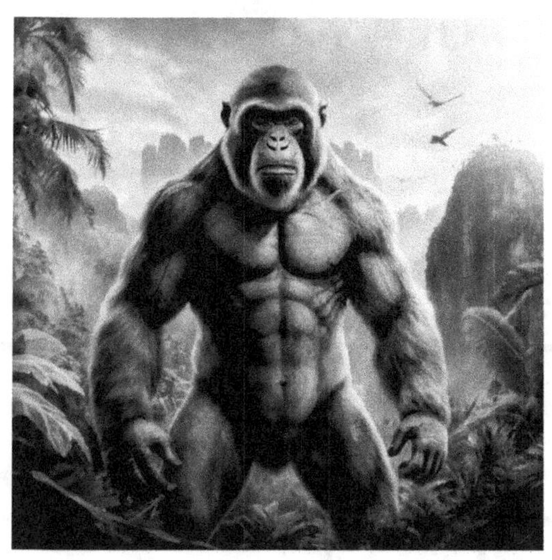 

Este livro pertence a:
This Book Belongs to:
這本書屬於：

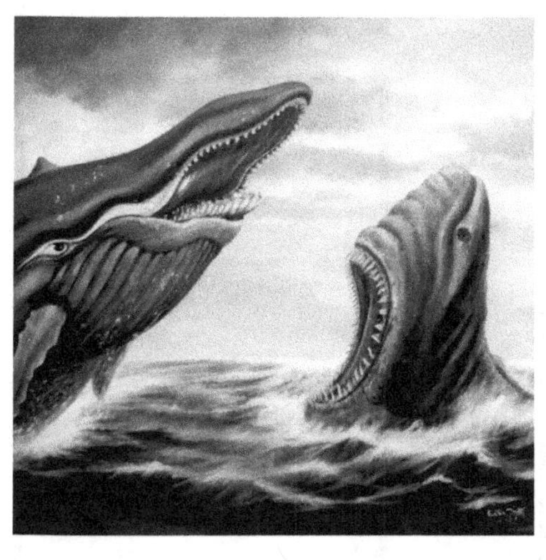 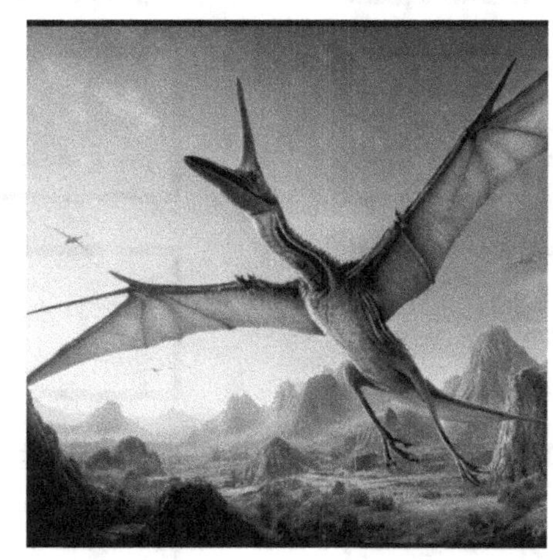

Test Color Page - 測試彩頁

Tyrannosaurus rex

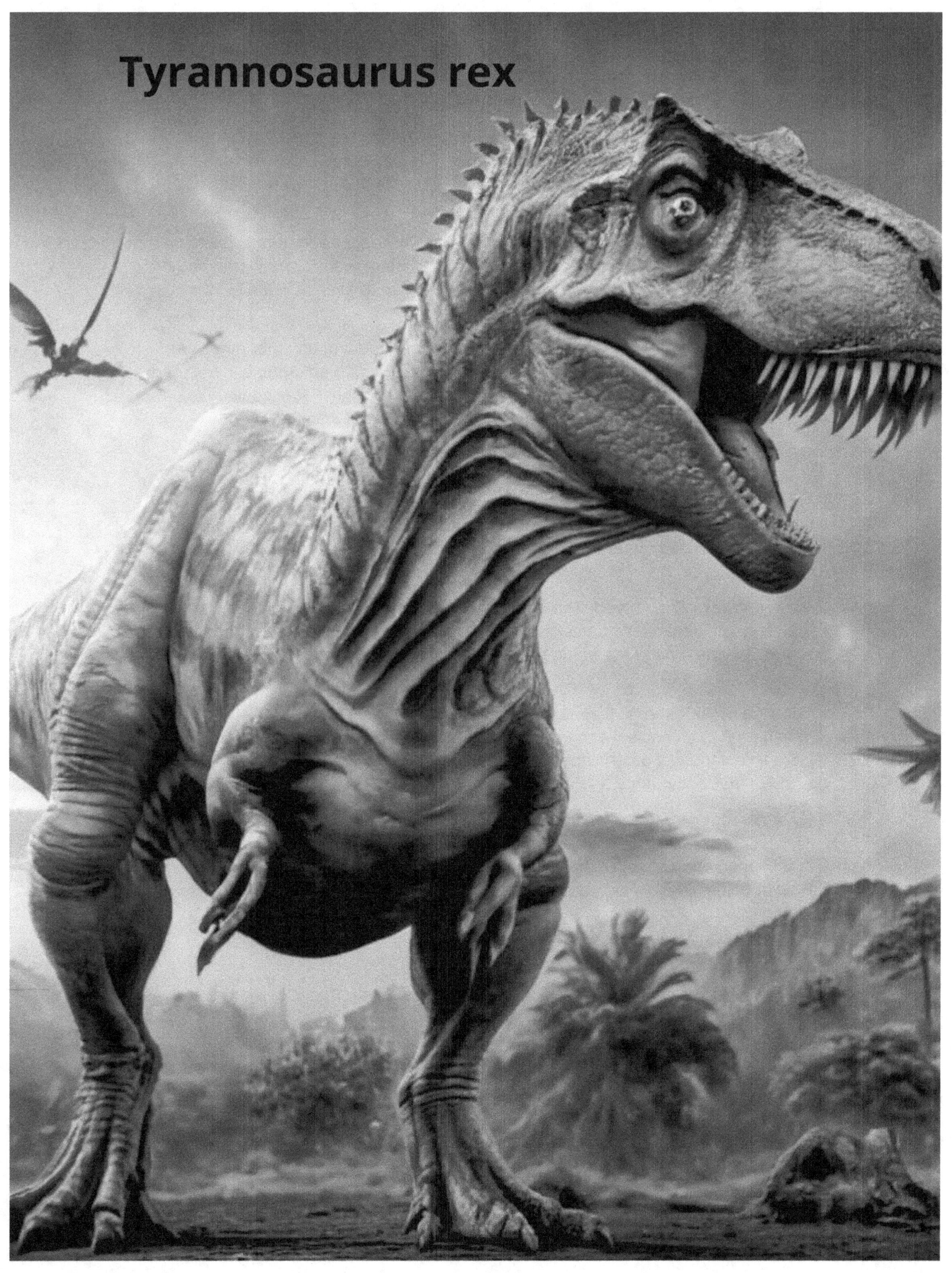

"The Mighty Tyrannosaurus Rex and His Ancient World"

Once upon a time, in a distant period called the Cretaceous, a giant reigned supreme among the dinosaurs: the fearsome Tyrannosaurus Rex, affectionately known as T-Rex. Let's explore the fascinating world of this king of reptiles!

The Imposing Appearance: The T-Rex was a true wonder of nature, with its massive structure and imposing head full of razor-sharp teeth. Its powerful body and balanced tail made it one of the largest predators to ever walk the Earth.

Food Habits: The T-Rex was a voracious carnivore, feeding on other dinosaurs. Its powerful jaw allowed it to crush bones, giving it a unique advantage in the food chain. Despite its predatory nature, studies suggest that the T-Rex could also be an opportunistic hunter, taking advantage of already dead animals.

How They Lived: The T-Rex's life wasn't just about fierce hunting. These giants shared surprising social characteristics. They could live in family groups, where they took care of the eggs and young. Their nests were true masterpieces of natural engineering, carefully constructed to protect precious future generations.

Places Where They Lived: The T-Rex roamed vast areas, from forests to plains, adapting to different environments. Its fossilized footprints have been found in several places around the world, revealing its striking presence in several regions.

The Age of Dinosaurs: By imagining the world of Tyrannosaurus Rex, we are transported to an ancient and mysterious era. These giants coexisted with an incredible variety of other dinosaur species, each contributing to the complex web of life in that distant time.

Kids, get ready for an adventure through time! Let's explore the majestic kingdom of the T-Rex and learn about its life, its exploits and the exciting age of dinosaurs that shaped our planet in extraordinary ways.
How about joining this journey and unlocking the secrets of Tyrannosaurus Rex?

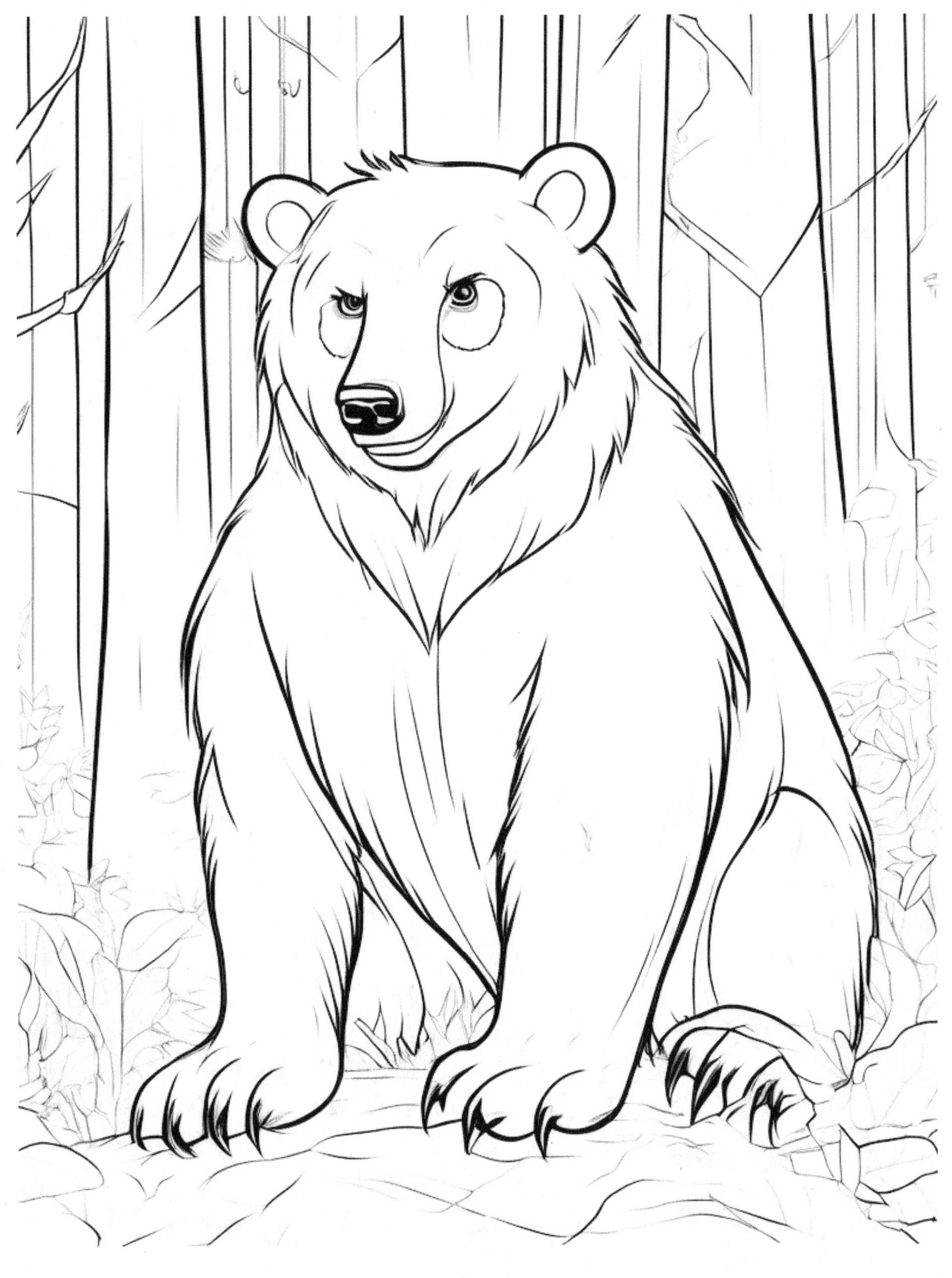

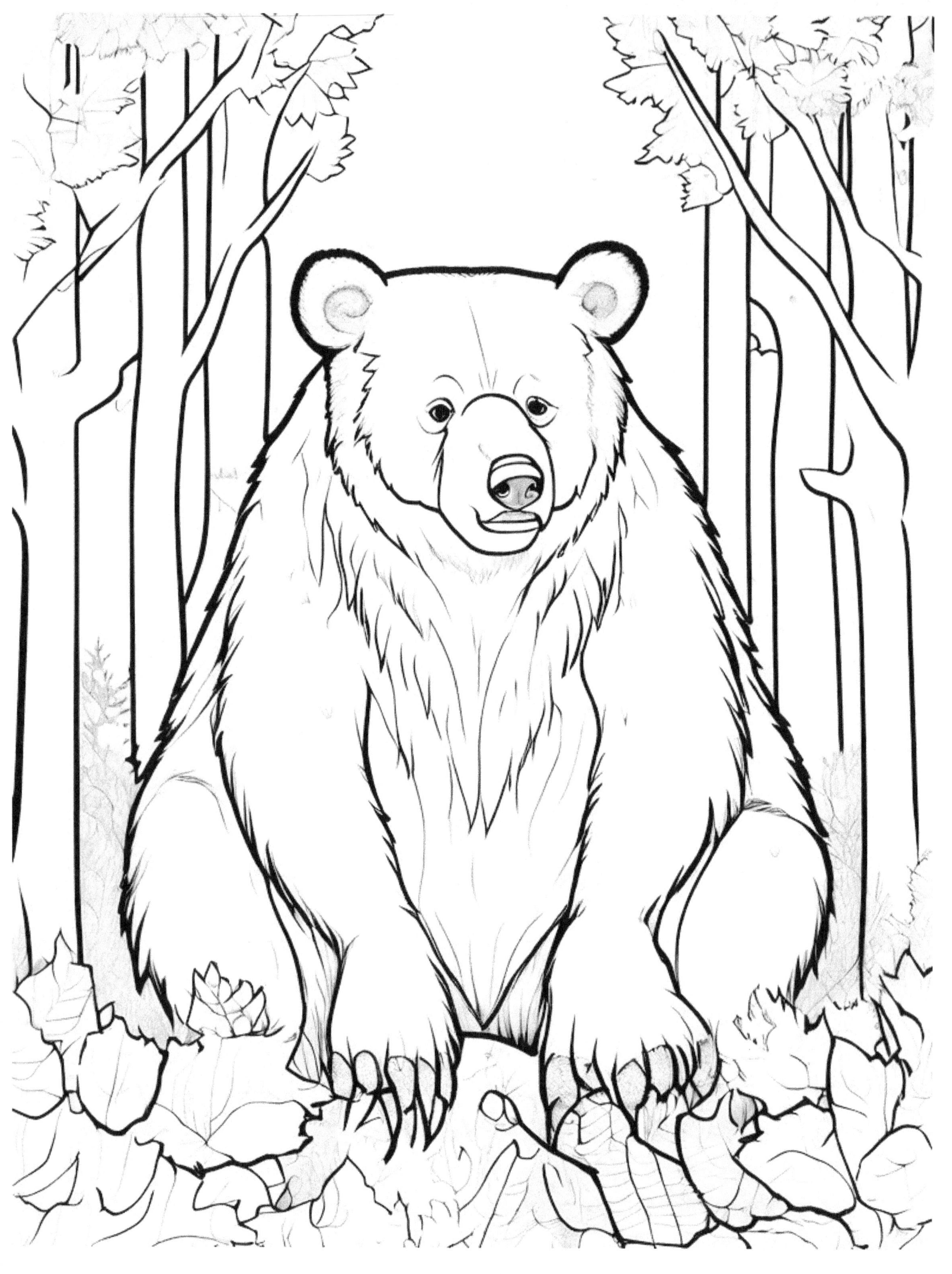

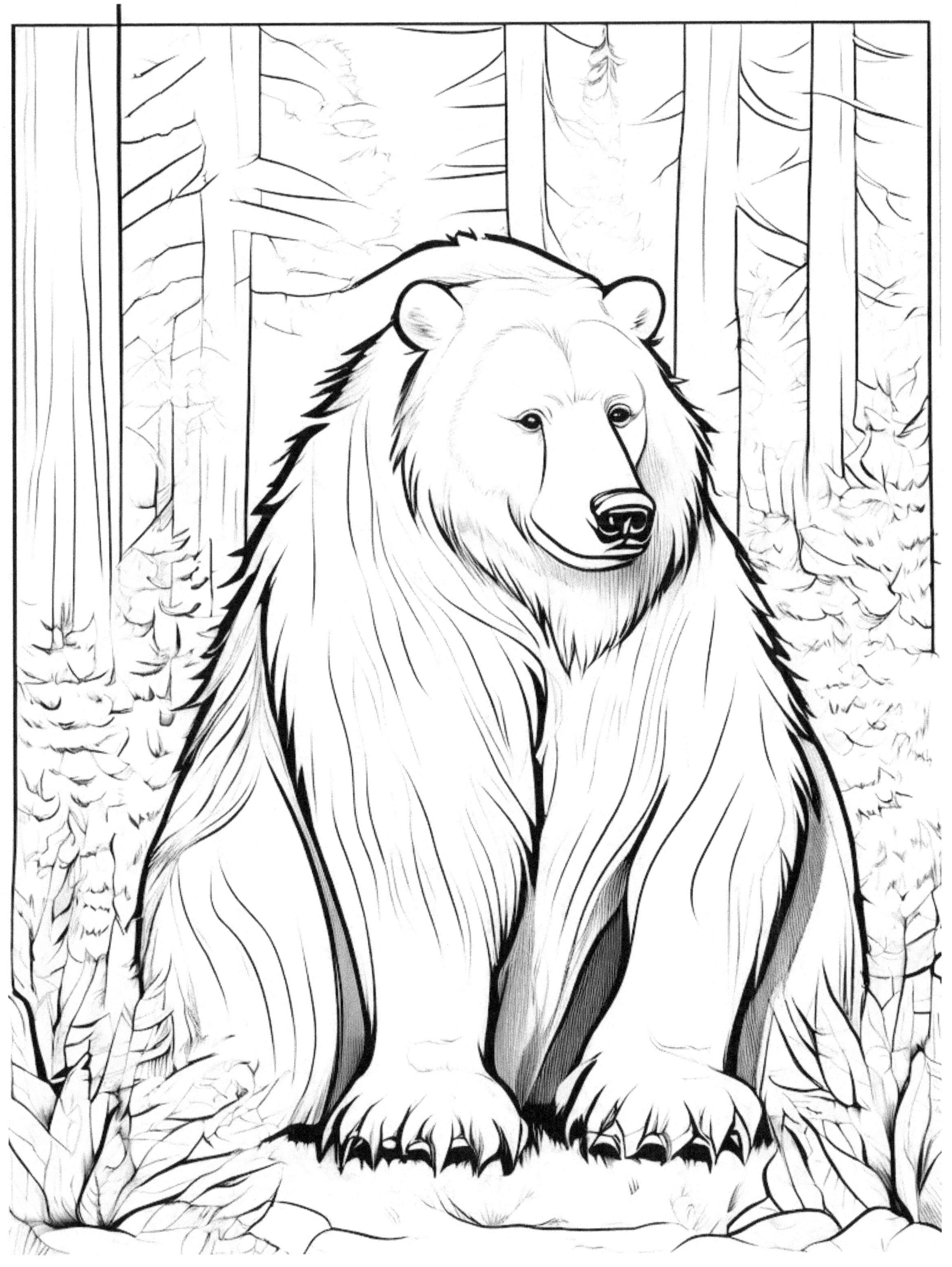

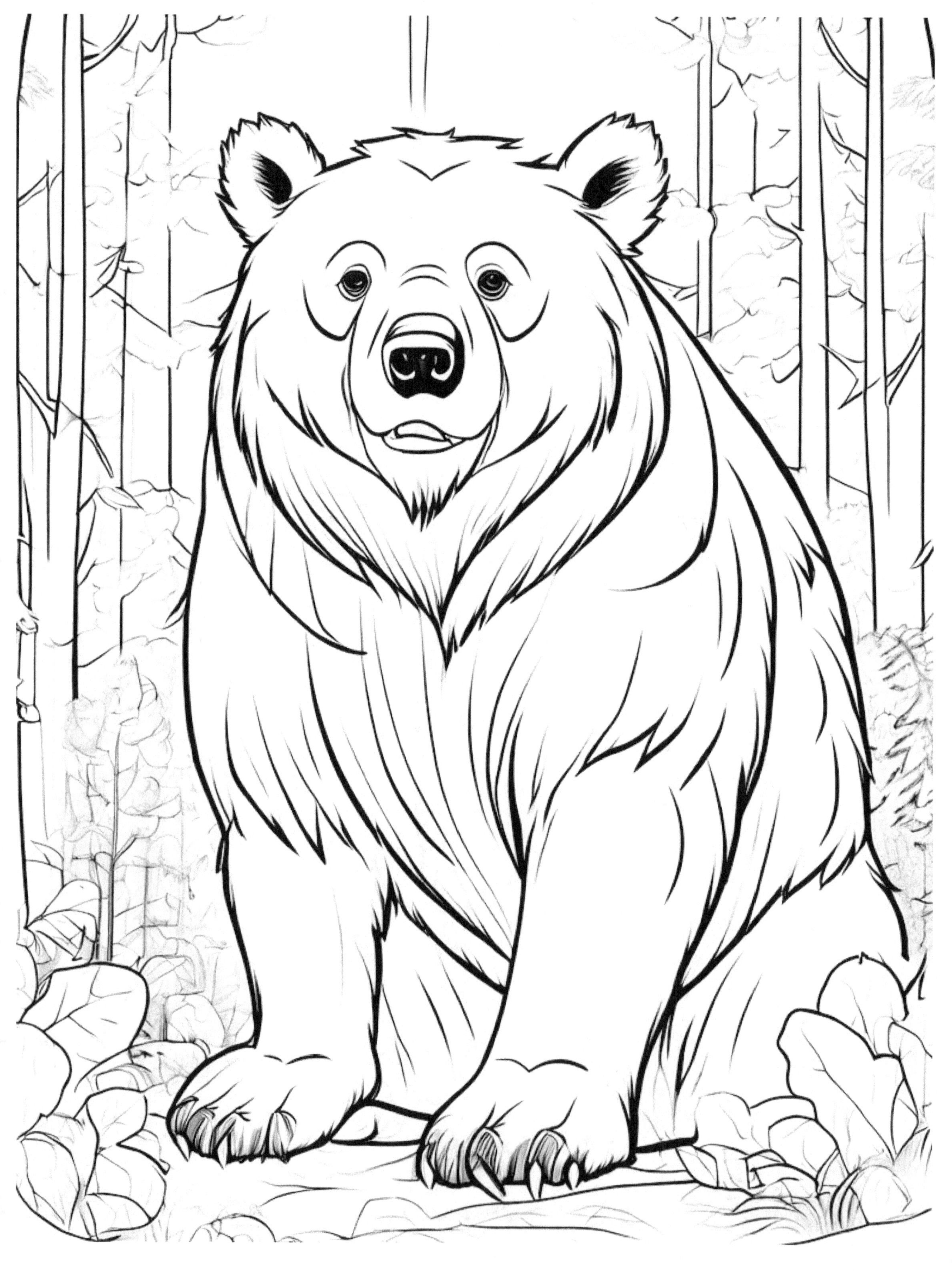

Title: "Arctodus: The Giant Ursid of Ages Past"

In the distant past, when vast expanses of land were ruled by magnificent creatures, a giant ursid dominated the landscapes: Arctodus. Let's explore the wonders of this furry colossus that roamed the ancient ages.

The Magnificence of Arctodus: Imagine a bear of gigantic proportions, with thick fur and impressive claws. Arctodus was truly a giant ursid, standing out as one of the largest land carnivorous mammals of its time.

Food Habits and Powerful Hunting: Arctodus was a formidable carnivore, feeding on a variety of prey, including mammoths and other large mammals. Its sharp claws and powerful teeth made it a fearsome hunter in ancient landscapes.

Life in the Ancient Lands: These giant ursids inhabited various regions of North America, from dense forests to vast plains. Their adaptability to different environments made them masters of ancient lands, exploring vast expanses in search of food.

Places Where Arctodus Reigned: Fossils of Arctodus have been discovered in several parts of North America, indicating its dominant presence in ancient landscapes. Its fossil remains tell the story of an imposing predator that walked the ancient lands.

Imposing Height and Weight: Arctodus reached considerable heights when standing, reaching more than 3 meters. Their weight varied, but some individuals could weigh more than a ton. These dimensions made it an imposing presence in prehistoric landscapes.

Adventure with Arctodus: Adventurous kids, close your eyes and imagine yourself walking through the ancient lands alongside Arctodus. Envision this giant ursid roaming the ancient forests, a majestic figure in a lost world.

Join us on this exciting journey to explore the mysteries and wonders of Arctodus, the giant ursid of ages past, a creature that left a remarkable footprint on the history of life on Earth.

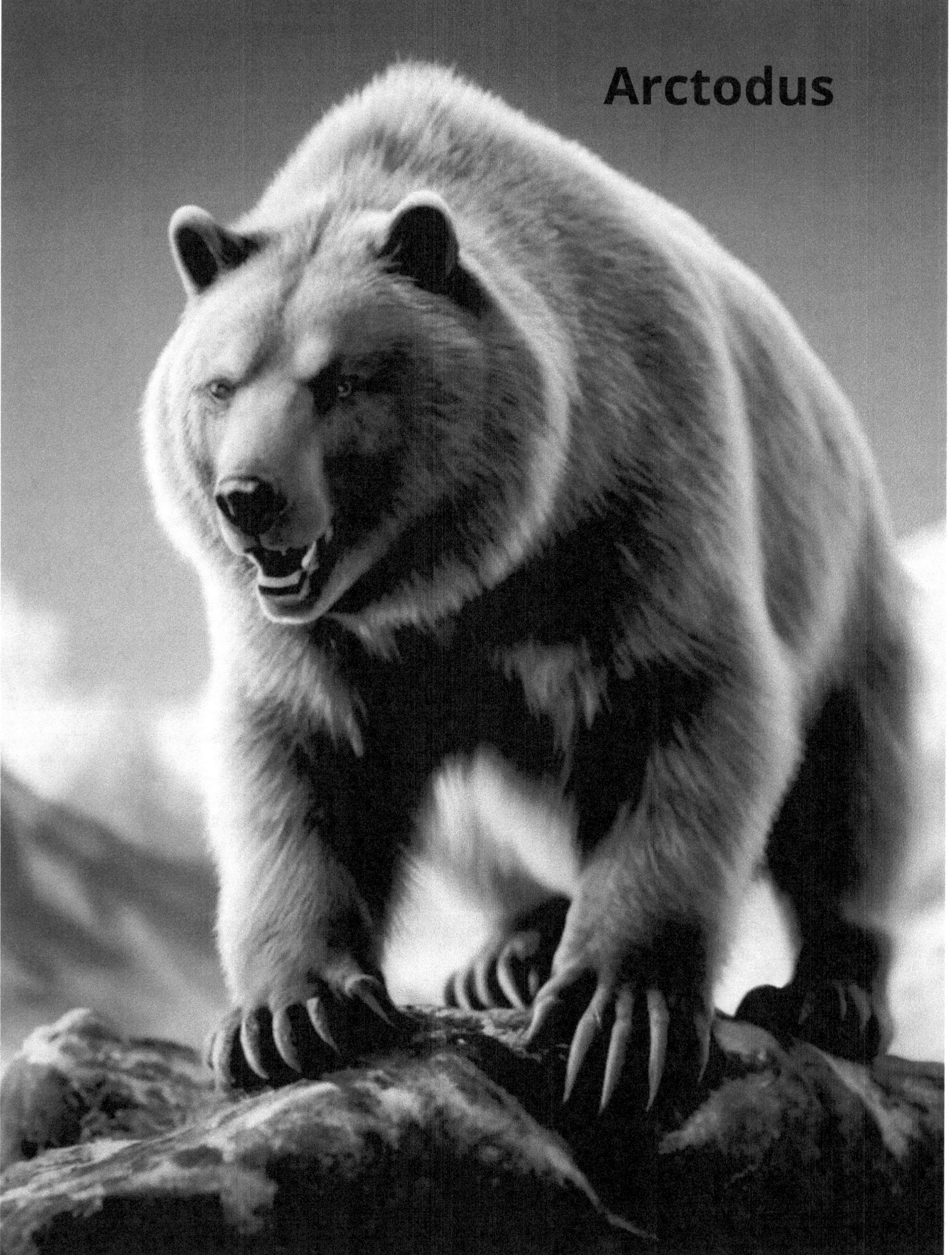
Arctodus

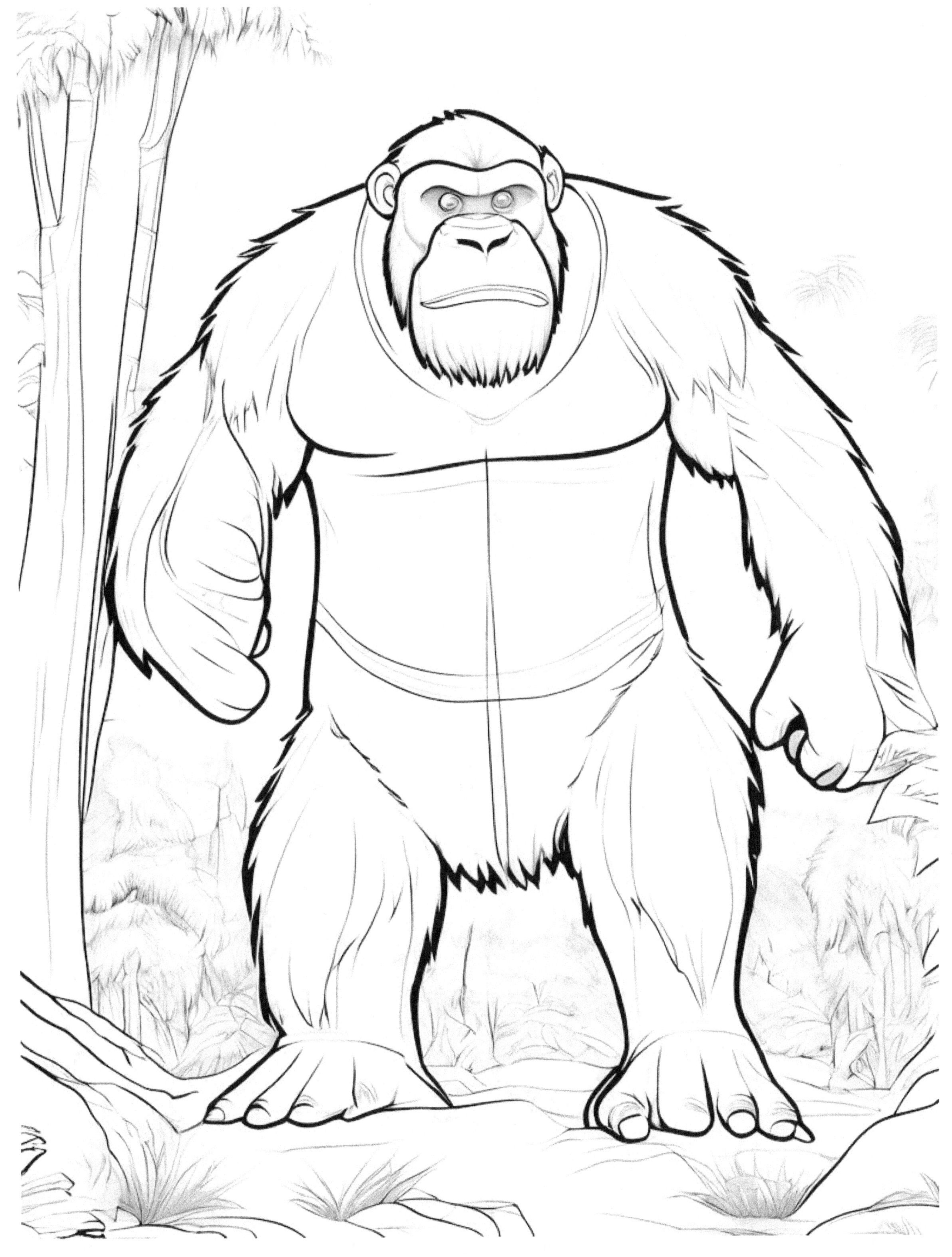

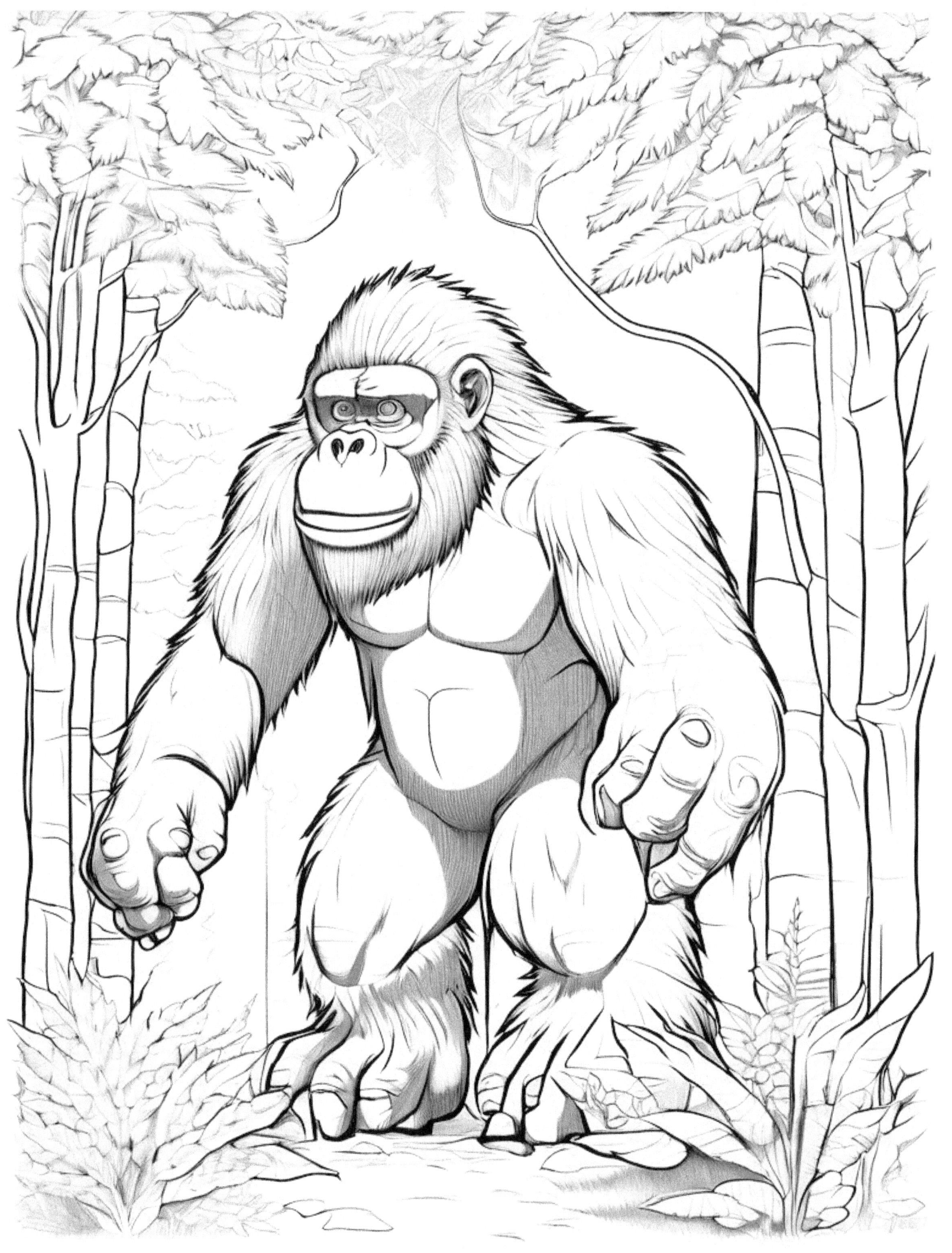

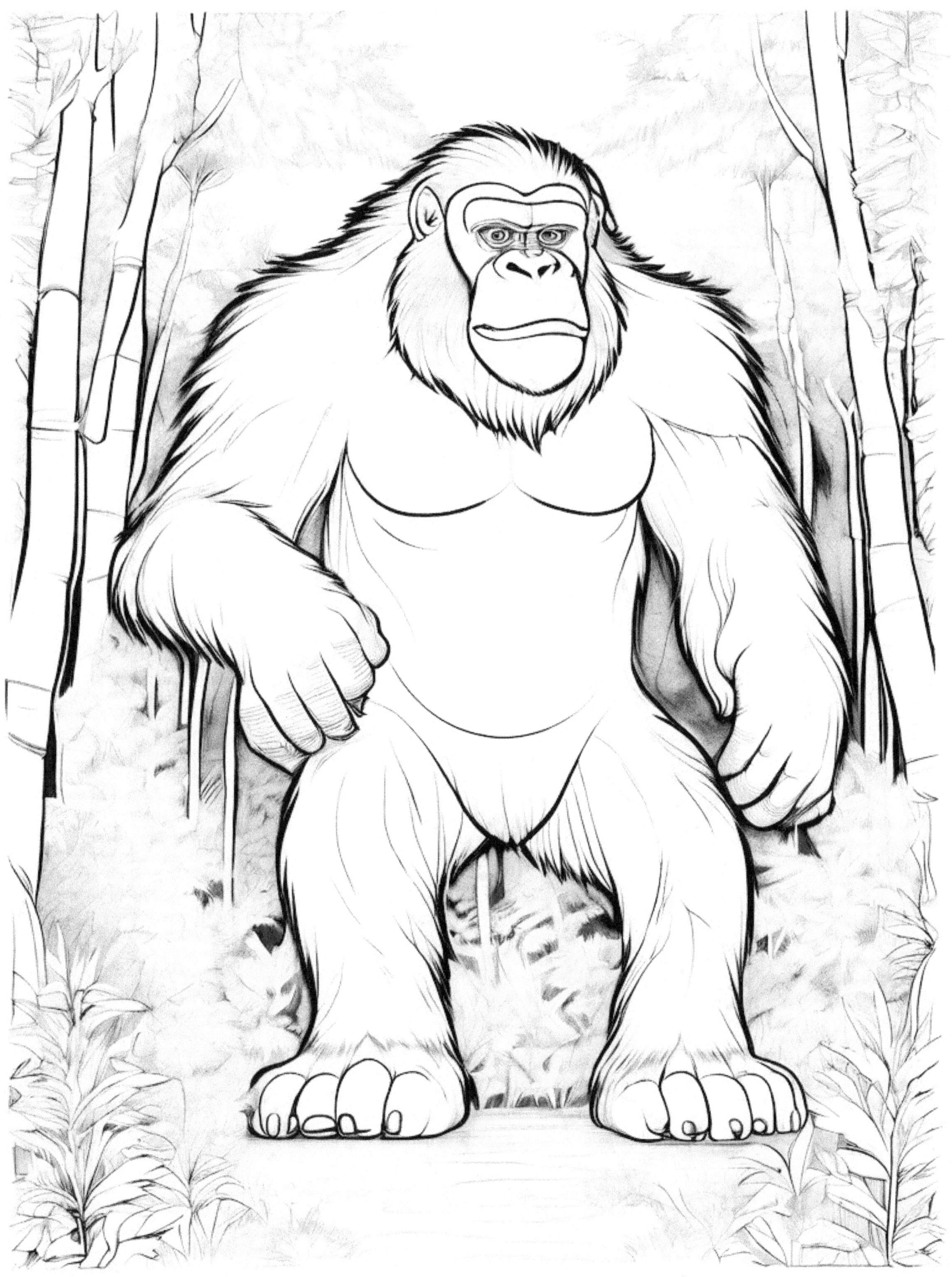

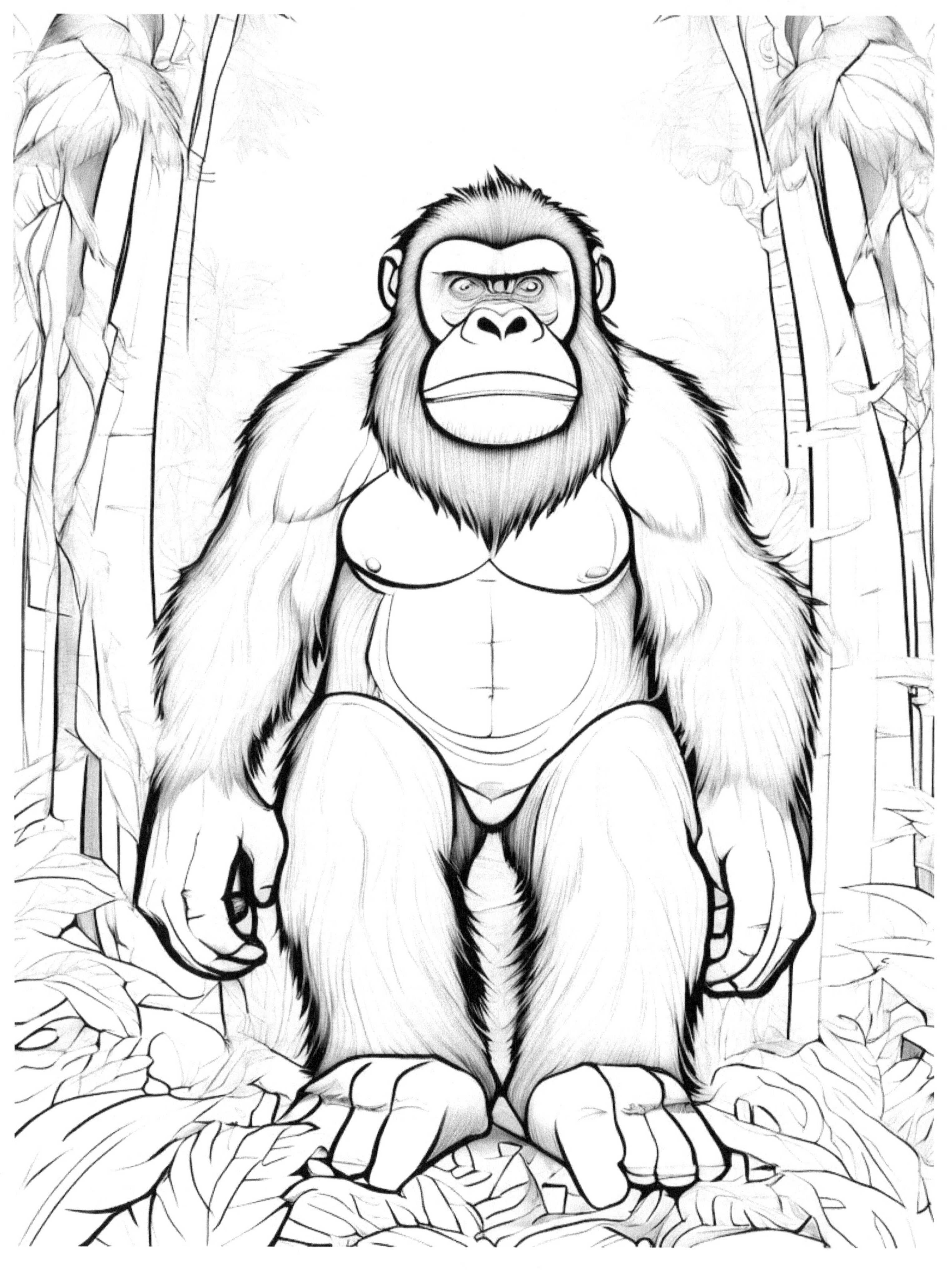

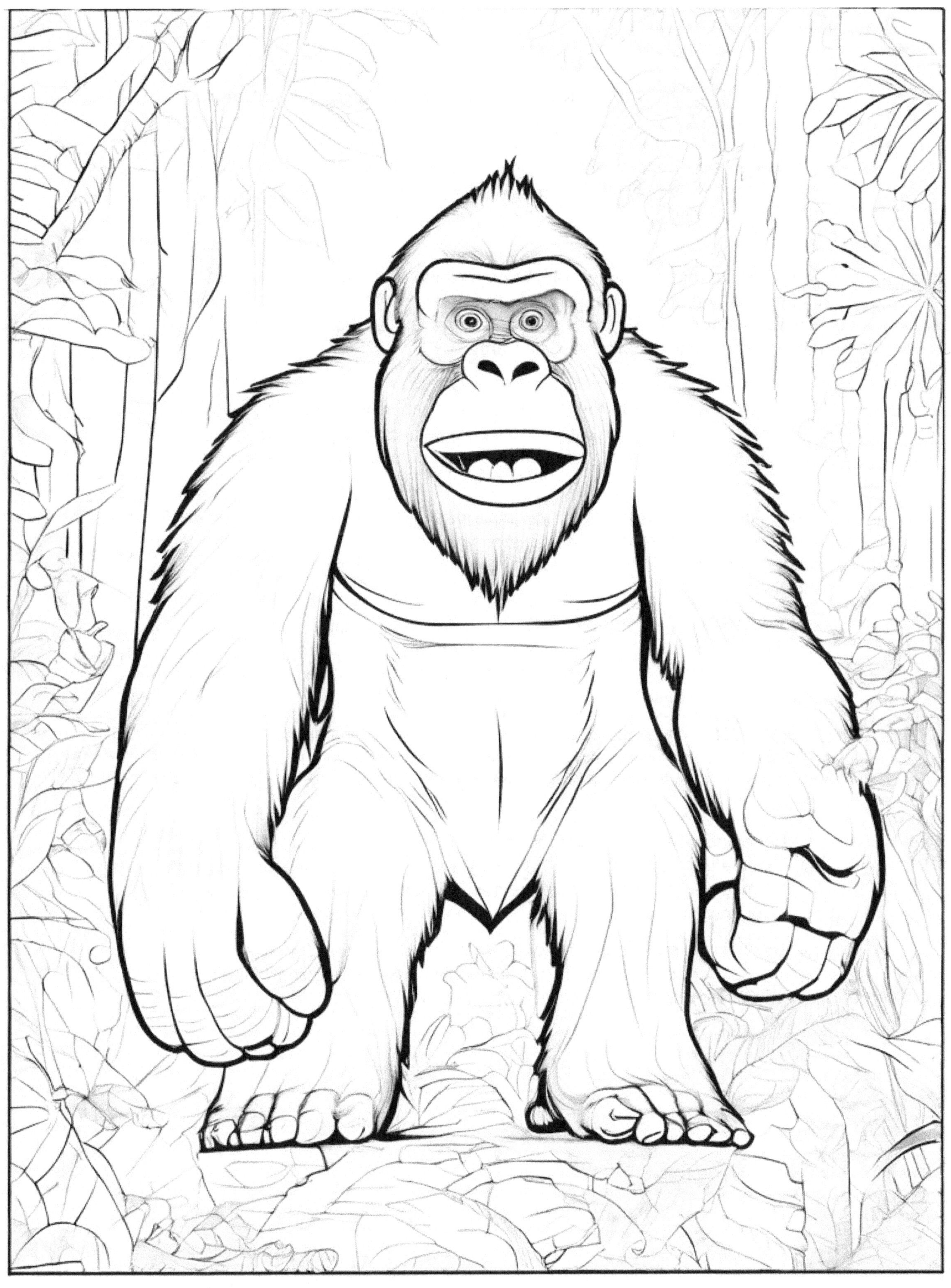

Title: "Gigantopithecus: The Giant of the Ancient Jungles"

In the distant past, when dense jungles covered vast expanses of the Earth, Gigantopithecus reigned like a giant among the trees. Let's embark on a journey through ancient jungles to uncover the secrets of this colossus of the past.

The Magnificence of Gigantopithecus: Imagine a primate of impressive proportions, with thick fur and an imposing presence.
Gigantopithecus was truly a giant of the ancient jungles, standing out as one of the largest primates to ever walk the Earth.

Food Habits and Vegetarian Diet: Despite its imposing stature, Gigantopithecus was a herbivore, feeding mainly on fruits, leaves and vegetation available in the jungles. Its vegetarian diet made it an important component of ancient ecosystems.

Life in Ancient Jungles: Gigantopithecus was an inhabitant of the jungles of Asia, roaming vast areas that would later become China, India and Vietnam. His adaptability to different jungle environments made him an intrepid explorer of ancient landscapes.

Places Where Gigantopithecus Reigned: Fossils of Gigantopithecus have been found in various parts of Asia, indicating their presence in different ecosystems. Its fossil remains tell the story of a colossal primate that roamed ancient jungles, leaving a lasting mark.

Imposing Height and Size: Gigantopithecus was truly gigantic, with some individuals reaching heights of up to 3 meters when in an upright position. Its size made it one of the largest primates in history, a true king of the heights in ancient jungles.

Jungle Adventure with Gigantopithecus: Adventurous kids, close your eyes and imagine exploring the ancient jungles alongside Gigantopithecus. Visualize these gentle giants moving among the trees, contributing to the complexity and beauty of ancient ecosystems.

Join us on this exciting journey to discover the mysteries and wonders of Gigantopithecus, the giant of the ancient jungles, a majestic being who left a remarkable footprint on the history of life on Earth.

Gigantopithecus

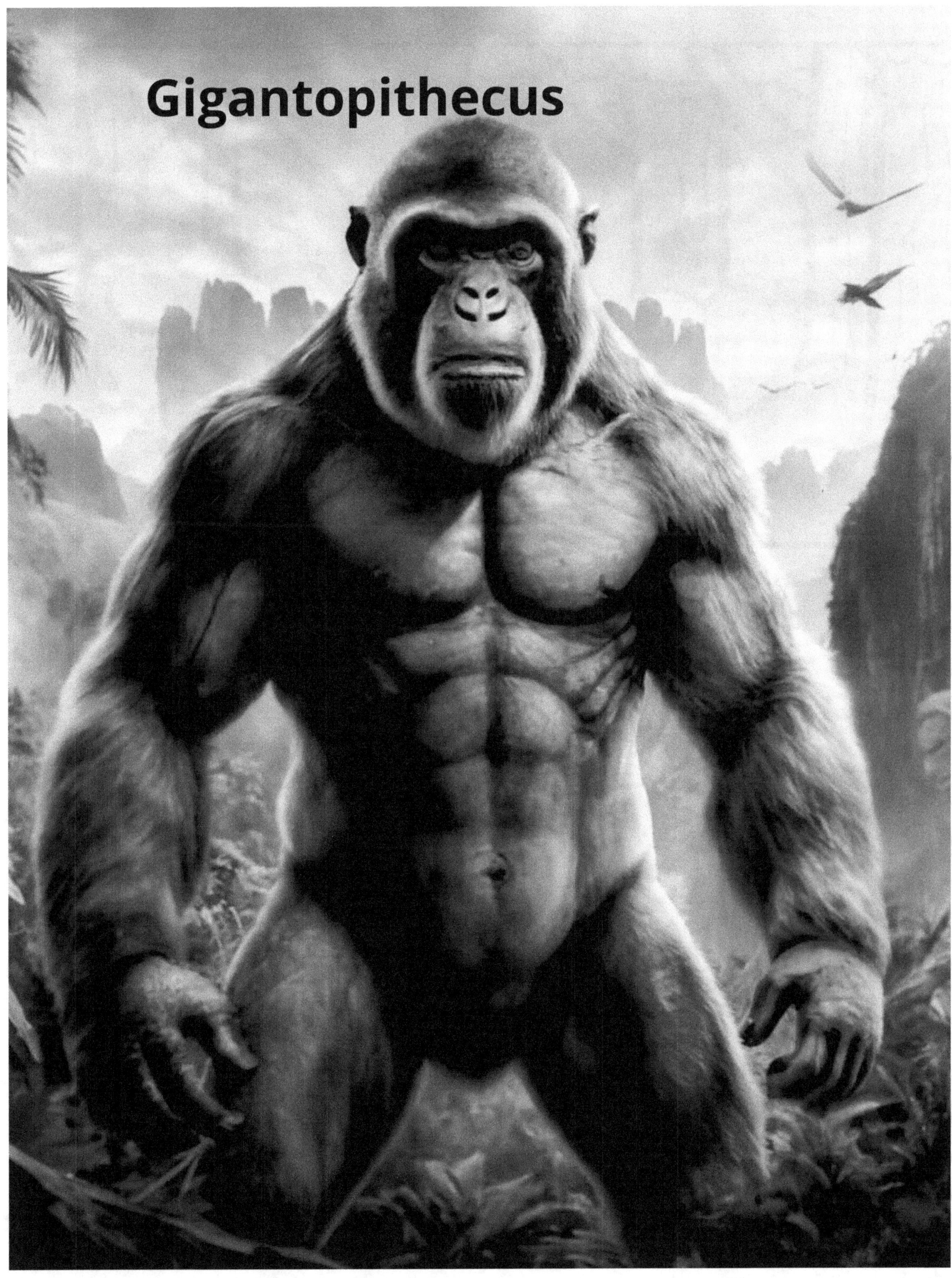

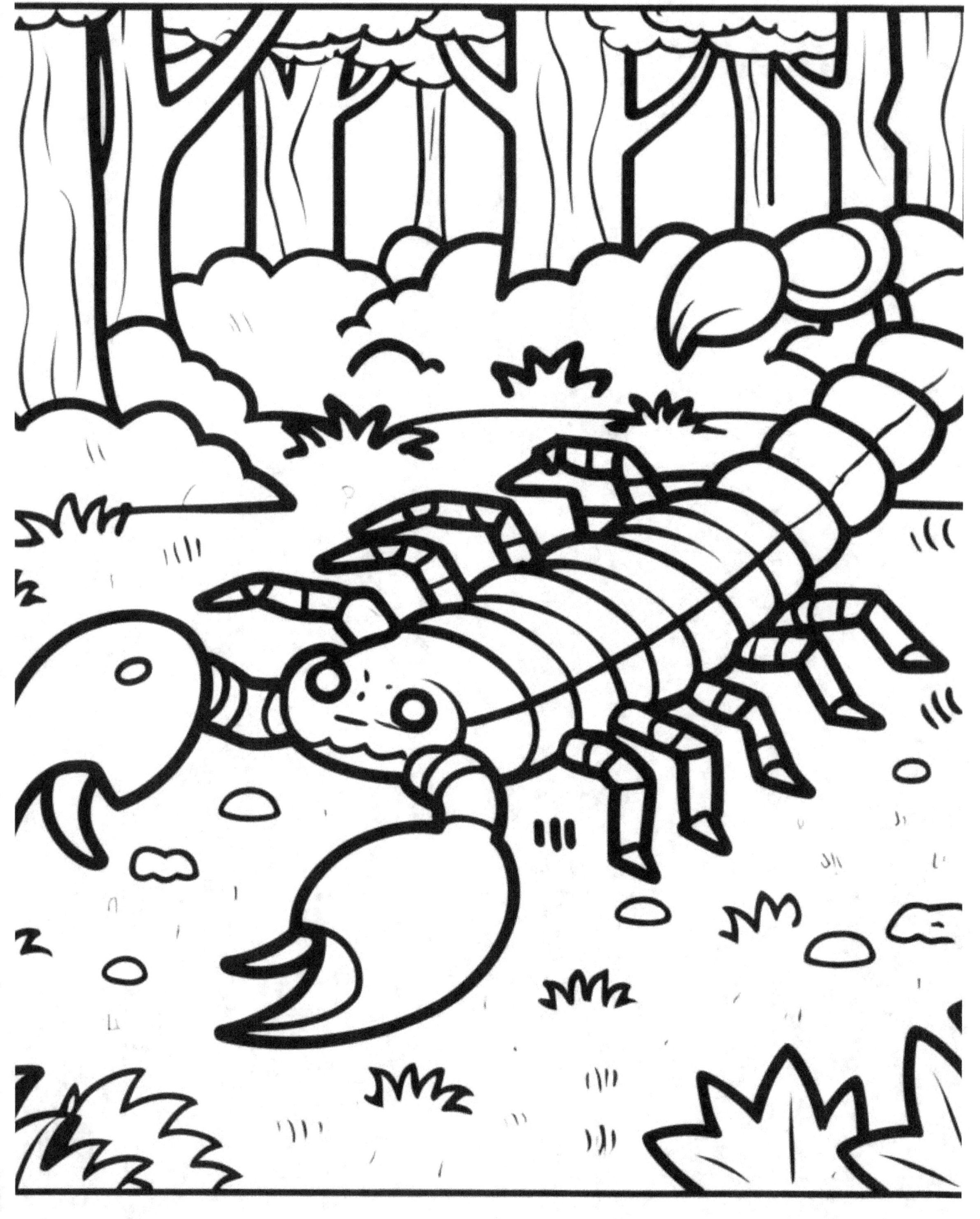

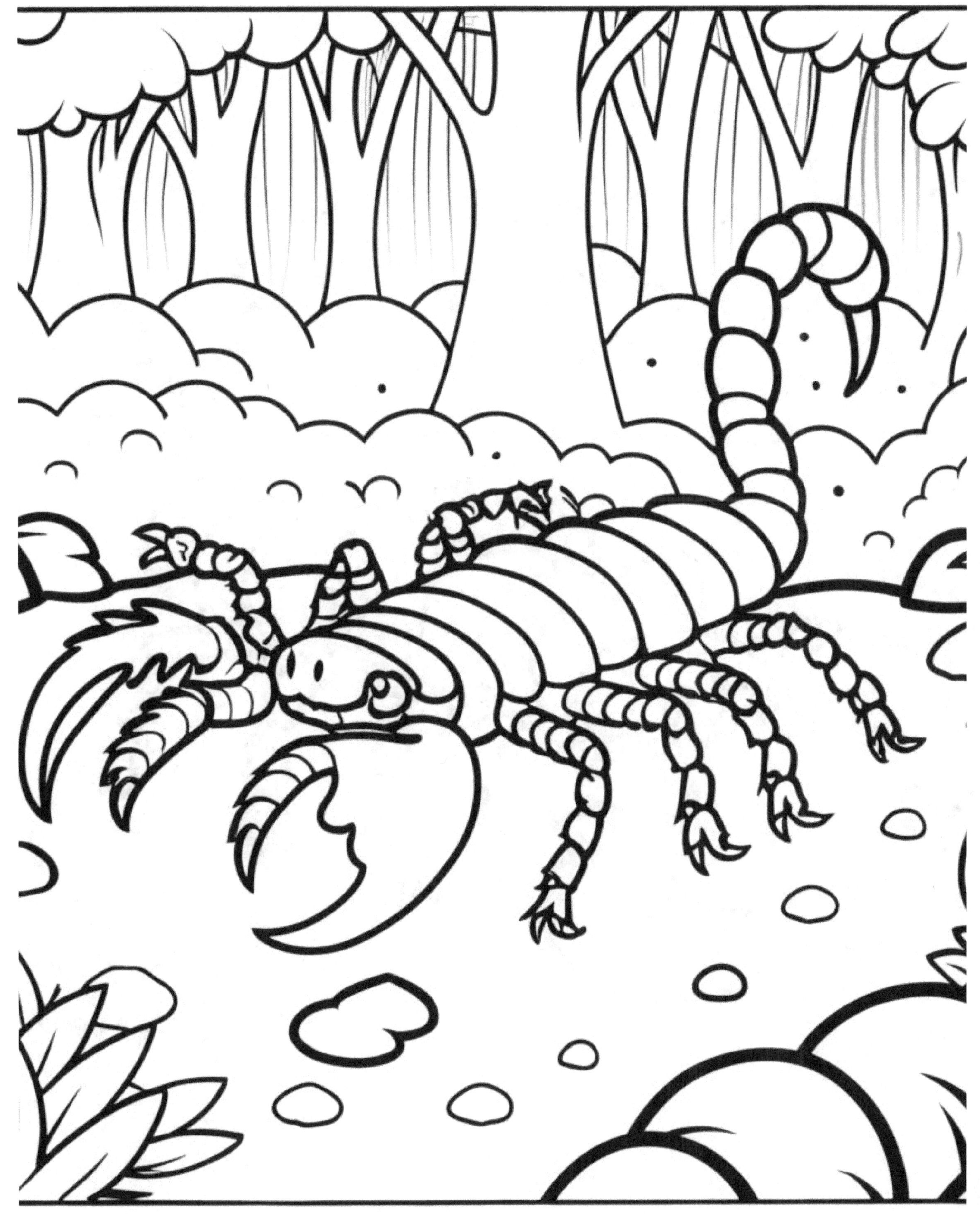

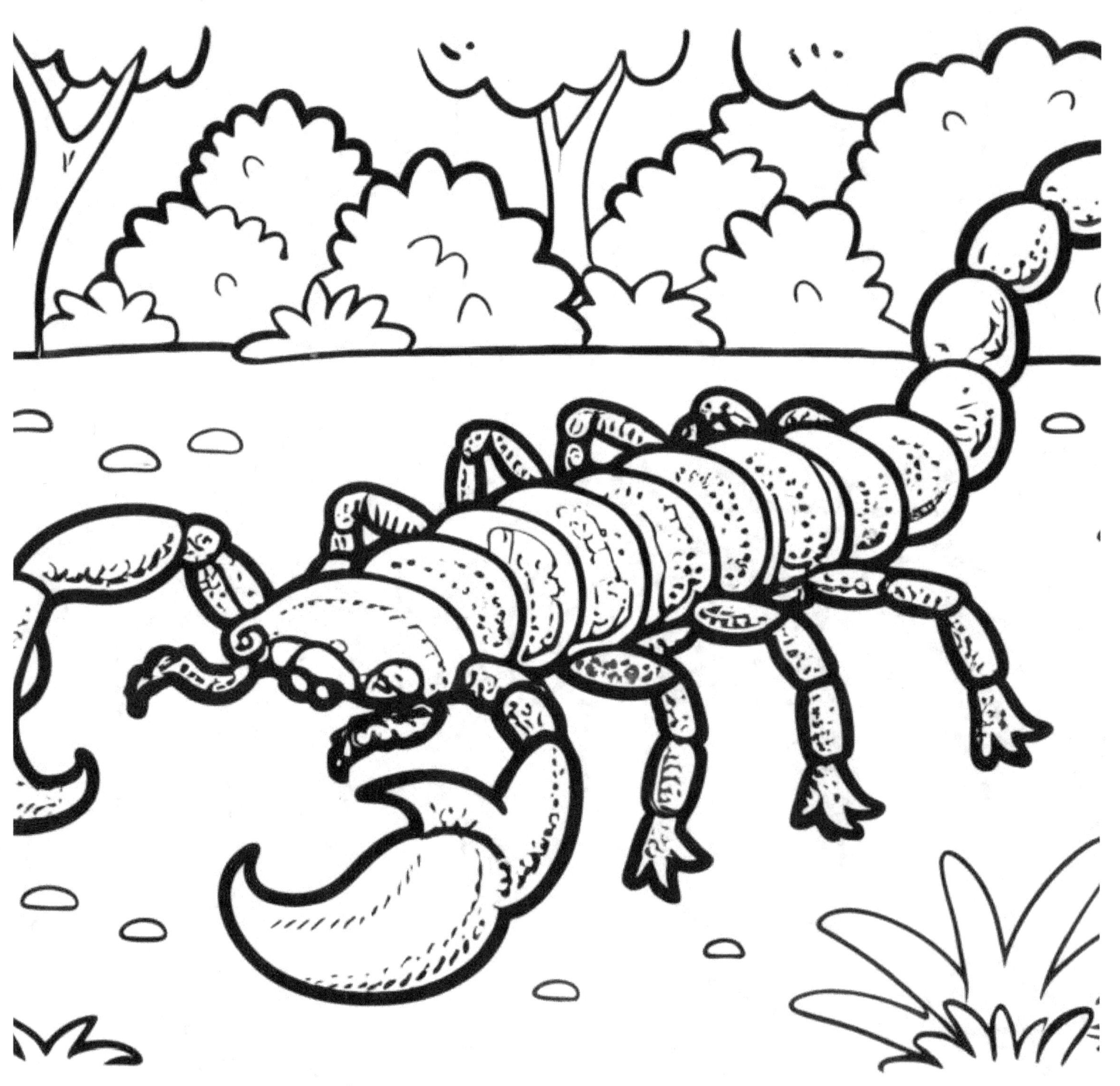

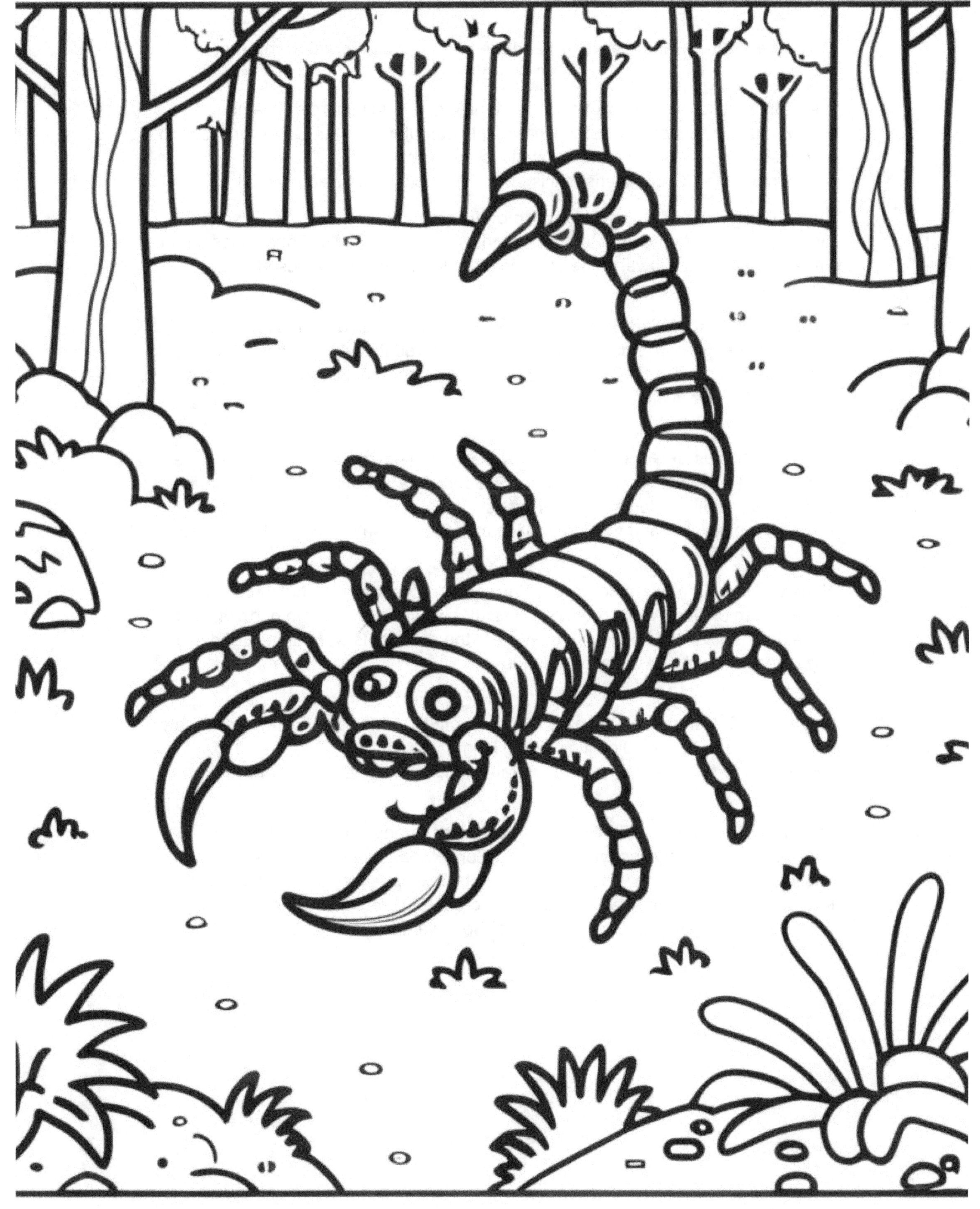

<h1 style="text-align:center">Title: "Gondwanascorpio emzantsiensis: The Ancient Guardian of Gondwana"</h1>

In ancient times, when the continents were united, a small guardian roamed Gondwana, the ancestral supercontinent. This guardian was the Gondwanascorpio emzantsiensis, an intriguing and mysterious creature.
Let's explore the life and deeds of this ancient inhabitant of ancient lands!

The Magnificence of Gondwanascorpio: Imagine a peculiar scorpion, with curved pincers and an exoskeleton adorned with unique details. Gondwanascorpio emzantsiensis was a jewel of the past, adapted to the vast territories of ancient Gondwana.

Food Habits and Skilled Hunting: This little guardian was a cunning hunter, feeding on the small insects and creatures that shared its habitat. Their delicate pincers were a precise tool for capturing their prey, demonstrating a remarkable adaptation to their ecology.

Life in the Lands of Gondwana: Gondwanascorpio emzantsiensis inhabited the vast lands of the ancient supercontinent of Gondwana. It could be found in varied landscapes, from lush forests to drier areas.
Its tough exoskeleton and hunting abilities made it a versatile and resilient inhabitant.

Places Where Gondwanascorpio Reigned: Gondwanascorpio emzantsiensis was a citizen of Gondwana, roaming areas that would later become parts of South Africa. Its fossils tell the story of a time when the continents were united, and this small creature explored the ancient lands.

Height and Dimensions: Compared to a person, Gondwanascorpio was relatively small, measuring about 10 centimeters in length.
Despite its modest size, it was an important piece in the puzzle of ancient life in Gondwana.

Adventure to the Past with Gondwanascorpio: Curious children, close your eyes and imagine traveling back in time to Gondwana. Visualize the lush landscapes, where Gondwanascorpio emzantsiensis patrolled like a little guardian. Join us on this fascinating adventure to explore the secrets and wonders of Gondwanascorpio, the ancient guardian of Gondwana!

Gondwanascorpio

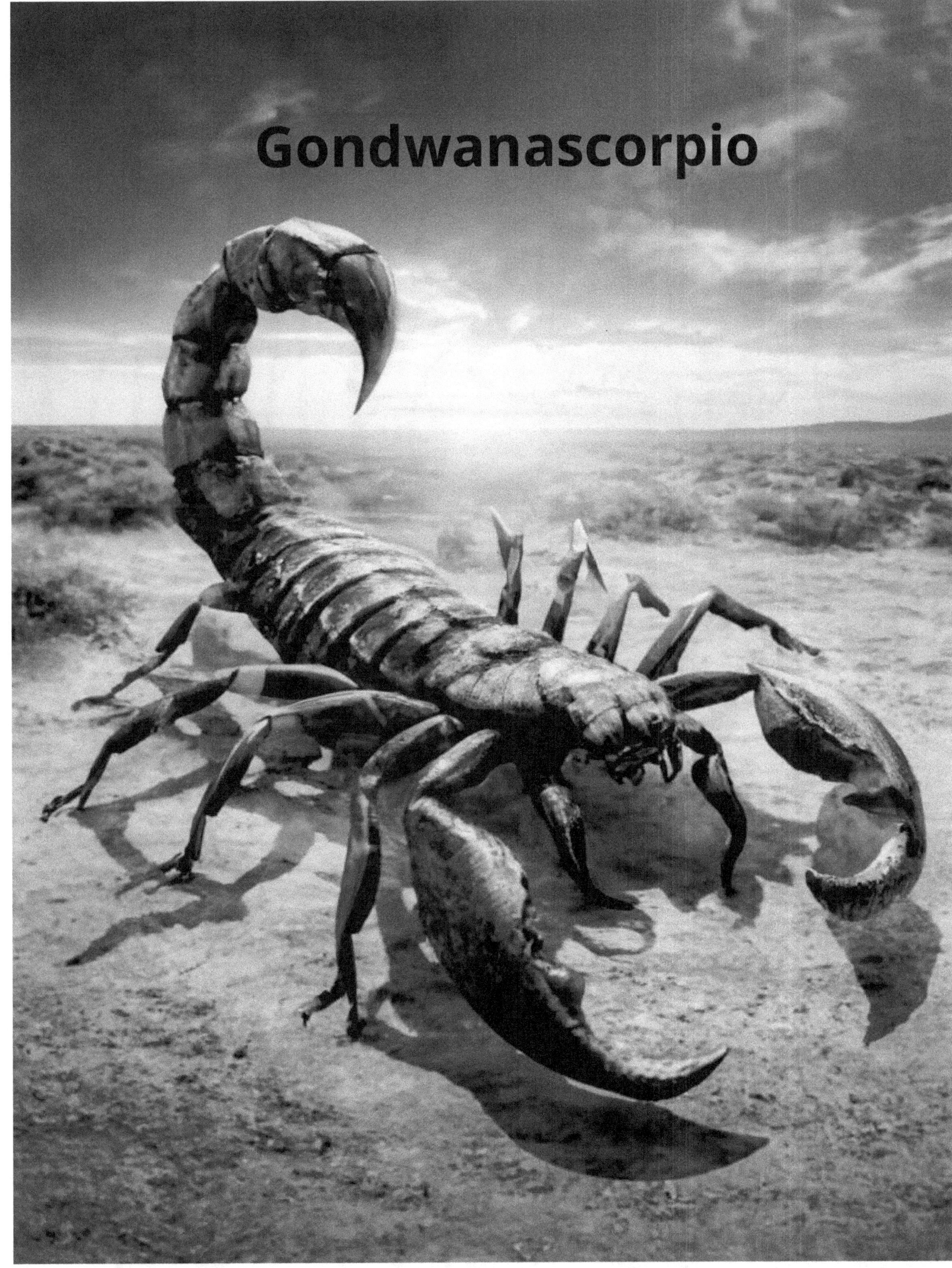

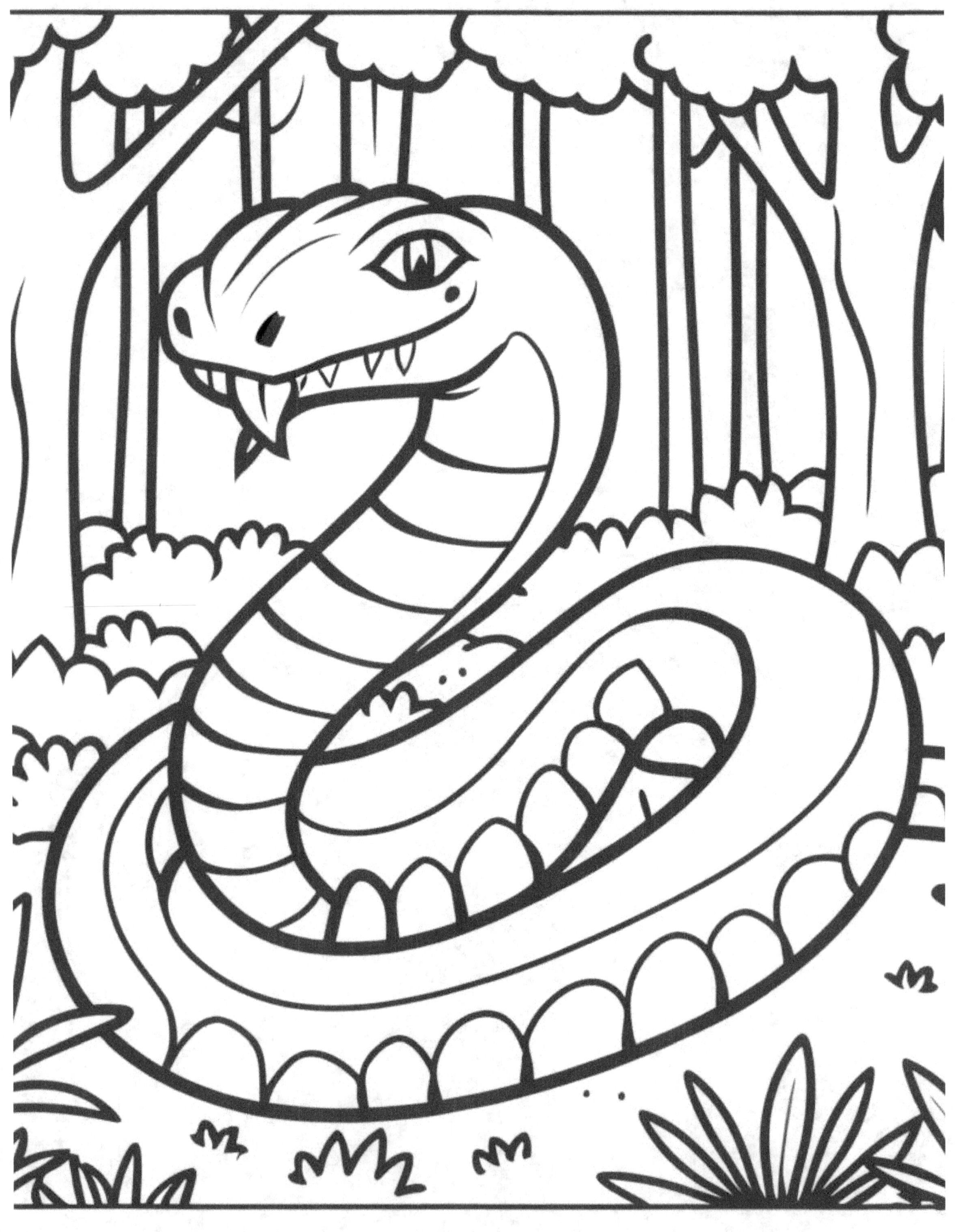

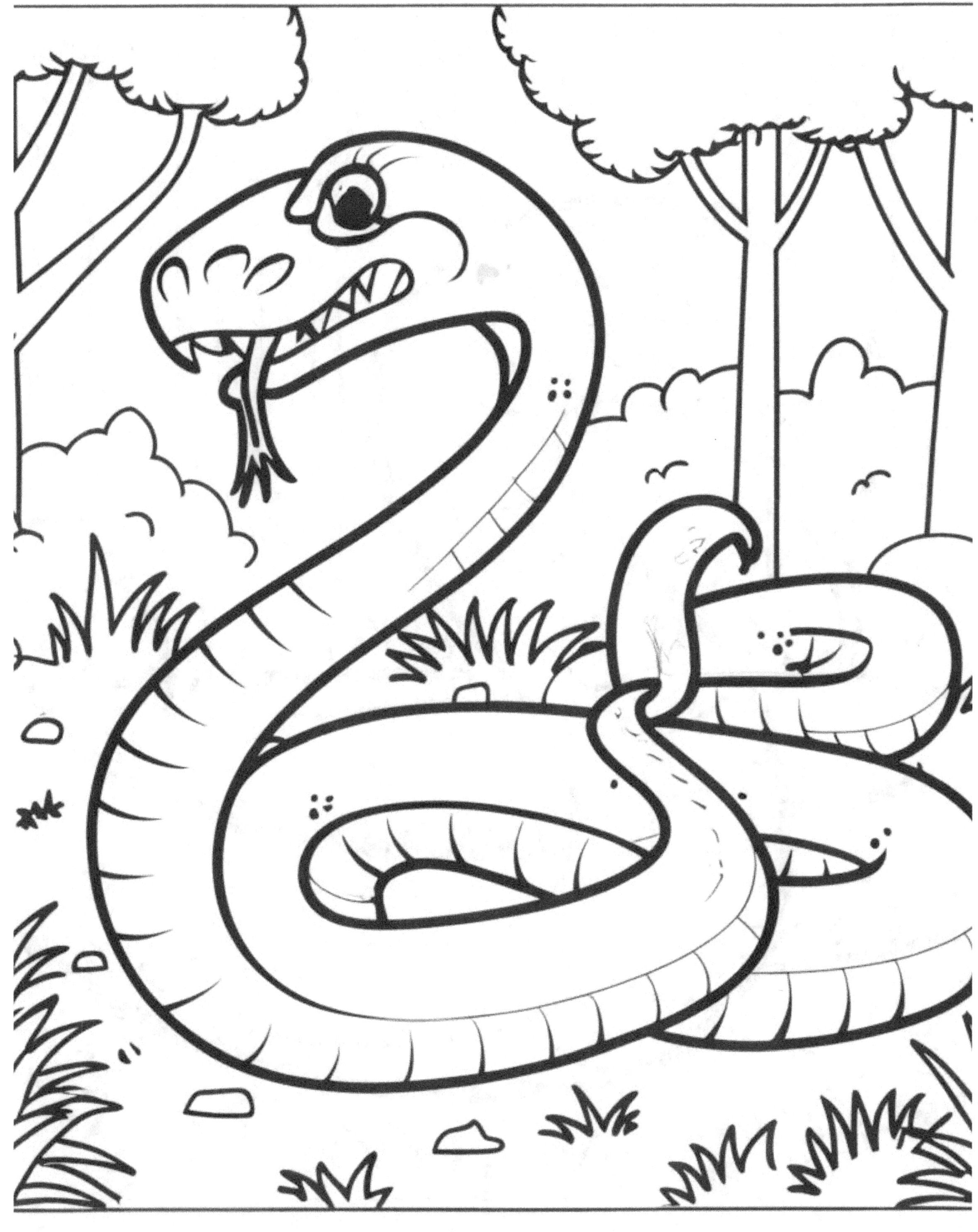

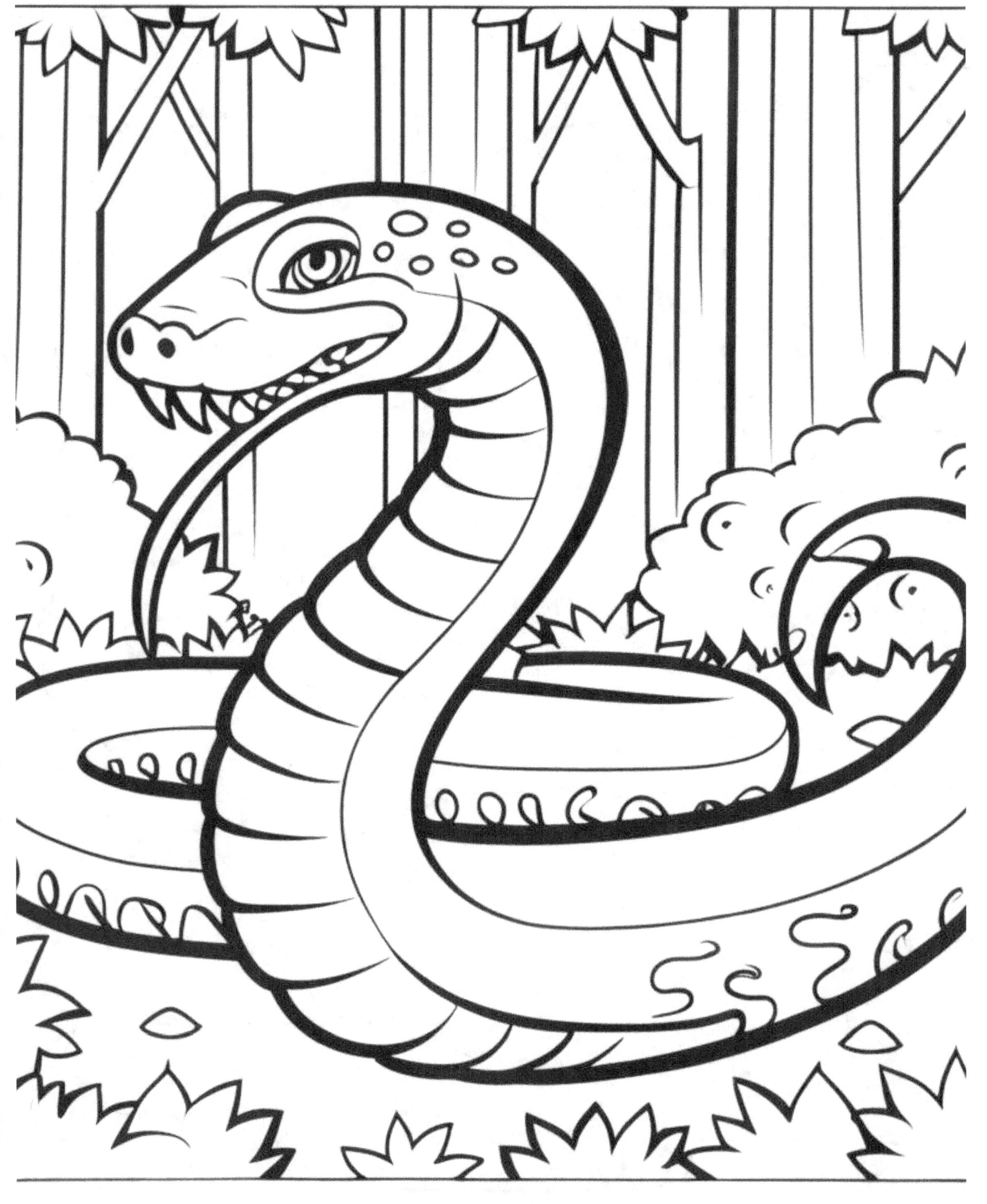

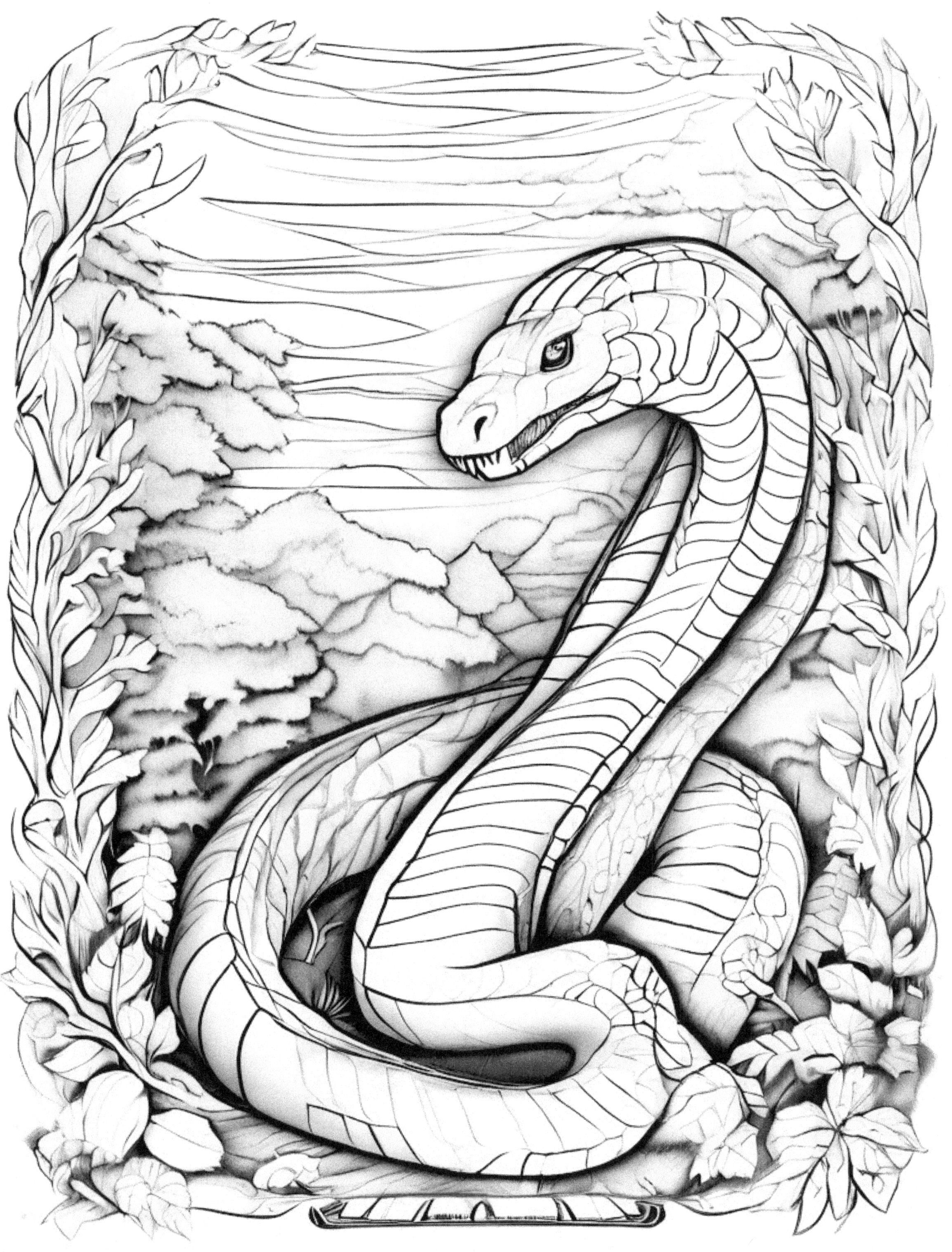

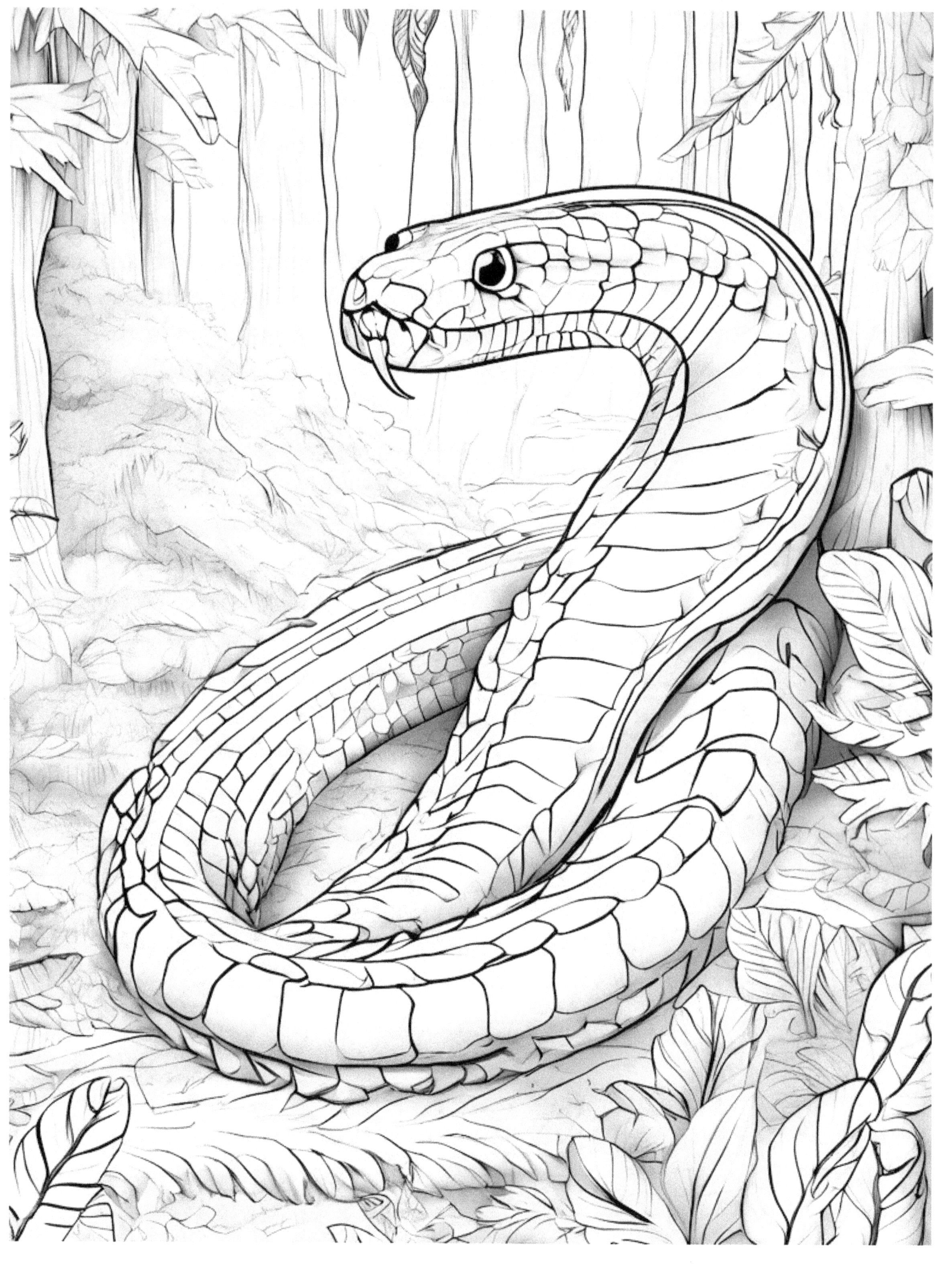

Title: "Titanoboa: The Colossal Serpent of the Prehistoric Swamps"

In the ancient past, when the swamps were vast and the rivers winding, an extraordinary creature glided through the waters: the Titanoboa. Let's explore the mysteries of these colossal serpents that ruled prehistoric ecosystems.

The Magnificence of Titanoboa: Visualize a colossal serpent, with an impressive length and a massive body that cut through the waters with grace. The Titanoboa was truly a wonder of nature, a giant serpent that defied all expectations.

Food Habits and Hunting in Water: The Titanoboa was a fearsome predator, feeding mainly on fish and other aquatic animals.
With its imposing size, it reigned as the top predator in its habitat, hunting strategically in the calm waters of prehistoric swamps.

Life in Prehistoric Swamps: These colossal serpents inhabited the swamps and rivers of South America at a time when the climate was warmer and wetter. Her massive body and swimming ability made her a master of aquatic environments.

Places Where Titanoboa Reigned: Titanoboa fossils have been discovered in Colombia, suggesting that these colossal serpents ruled the prehistoric swamps of South America. Their fossil remains tell the story of a time when the waters were ruled by giant predators.

Impressive Height and Weight: Titanoboa reached surprising lengths, reaching more than 12 meters. With its robust body, it could weigh more than a ton. These dimensions made it the largest snake known in history.

Aquatic Adventure with Titanoboa: Adventurous kids, close your eyes and imagine sailing through the prehistoric swamps alongside the Titanoboa. Visualize this colossal serpent gliding through the dark waters, a true ruler of ancient rivers.

Join us on this thrilling adventure to explore the mysteries and wonders of the Titanoboa, the colossal serpent of the prehistoric swamps, a creature that has left a lasting mark on the history of life on Earth.

Titanoboa

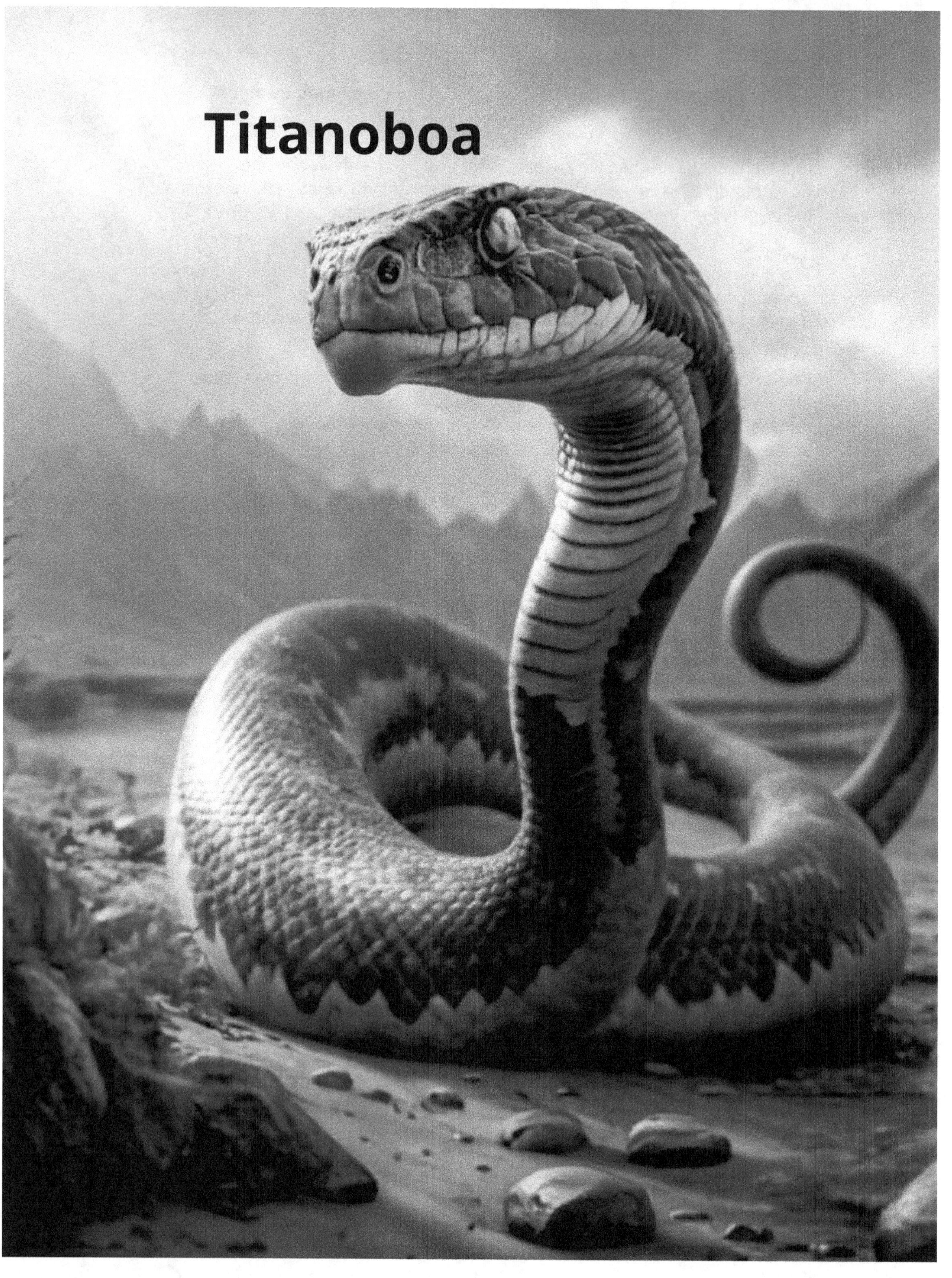

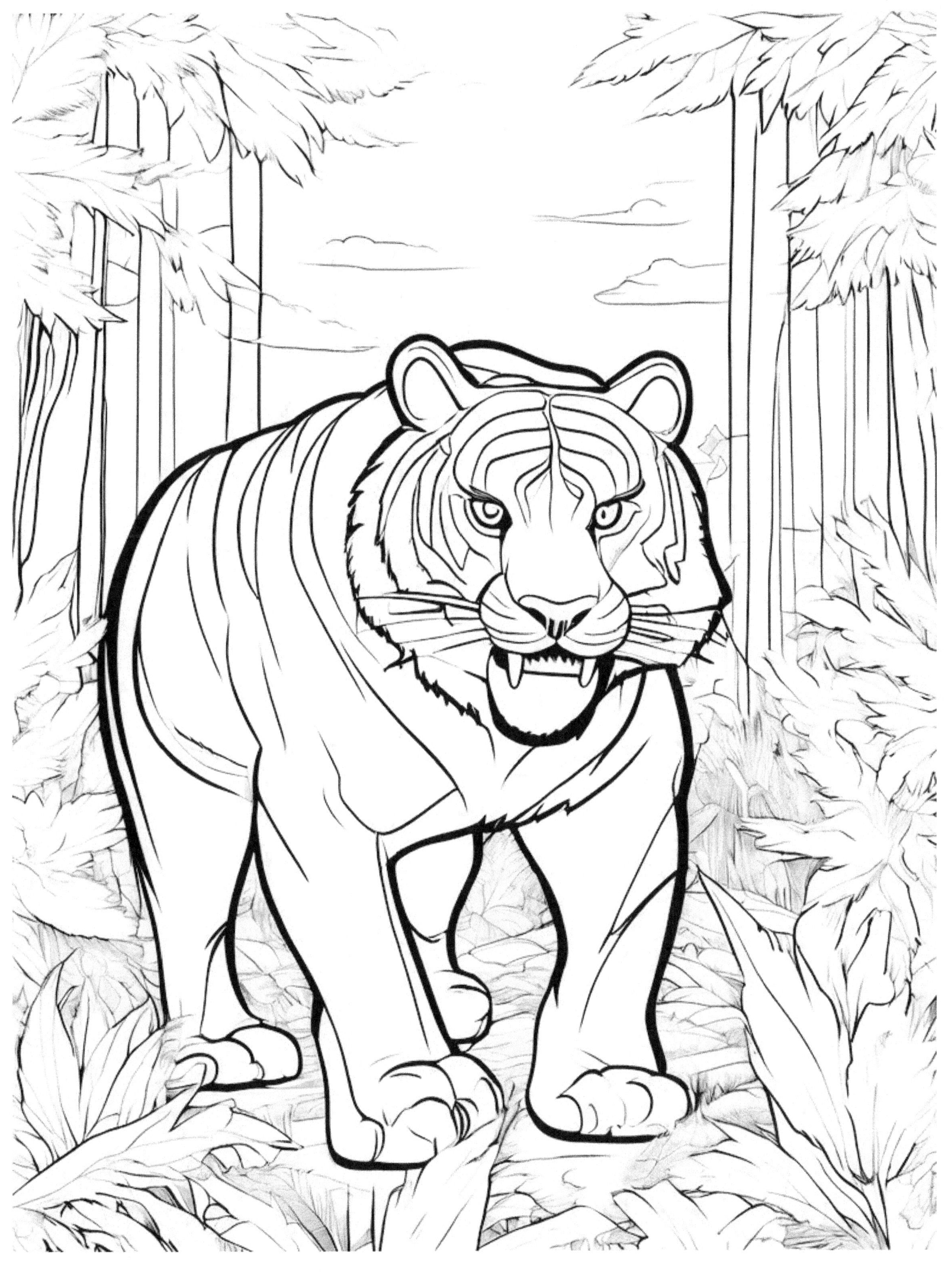

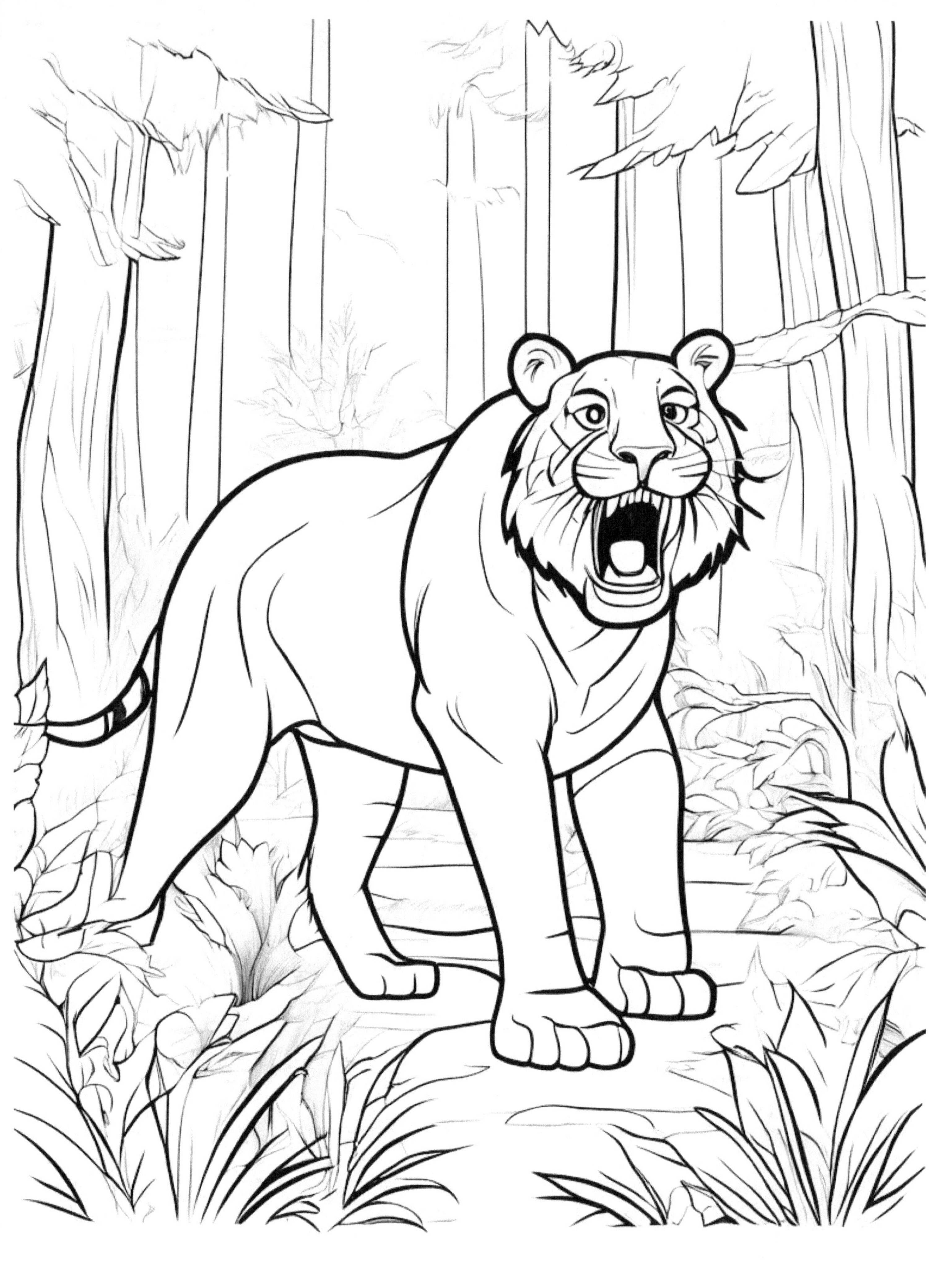

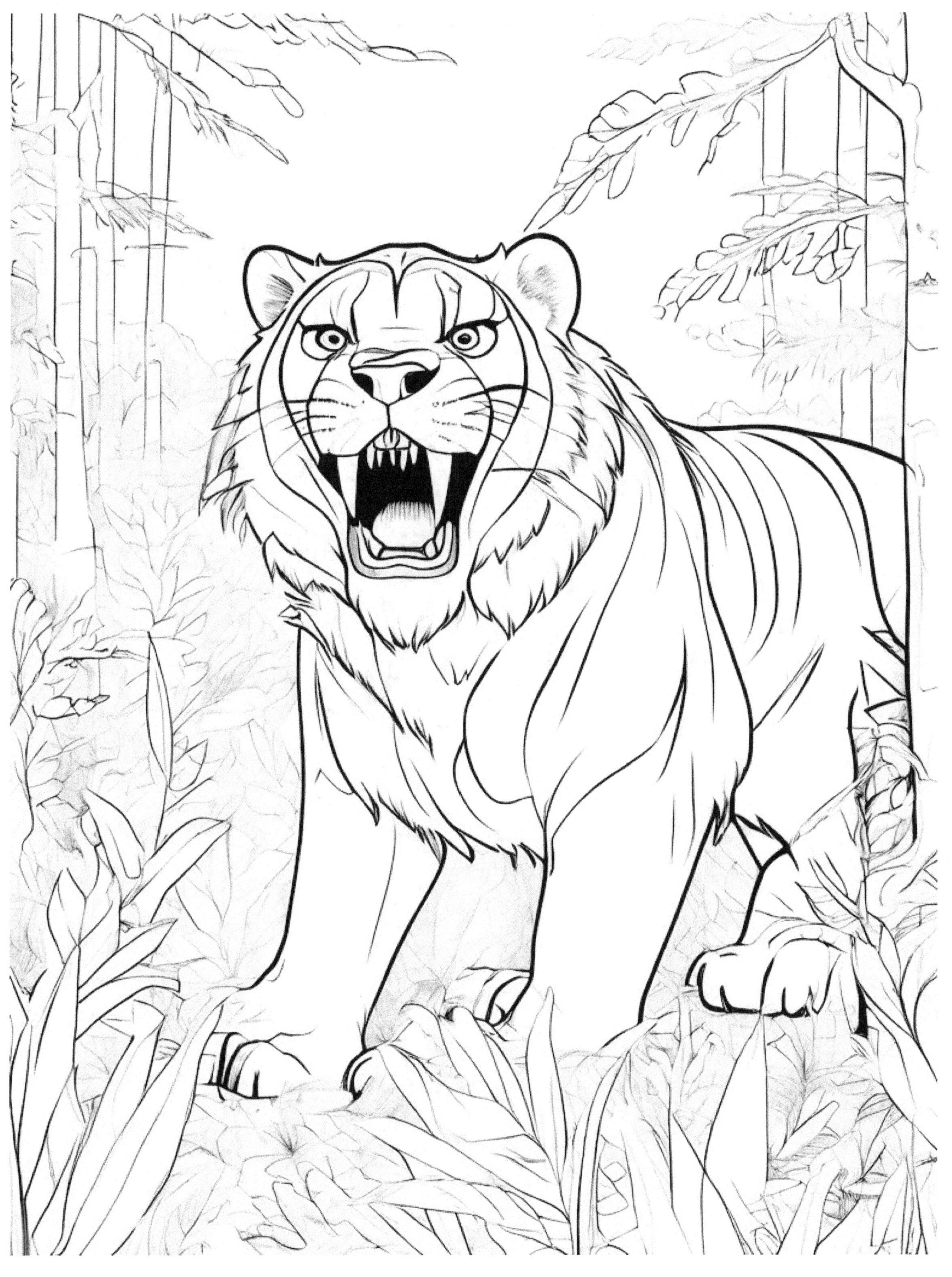

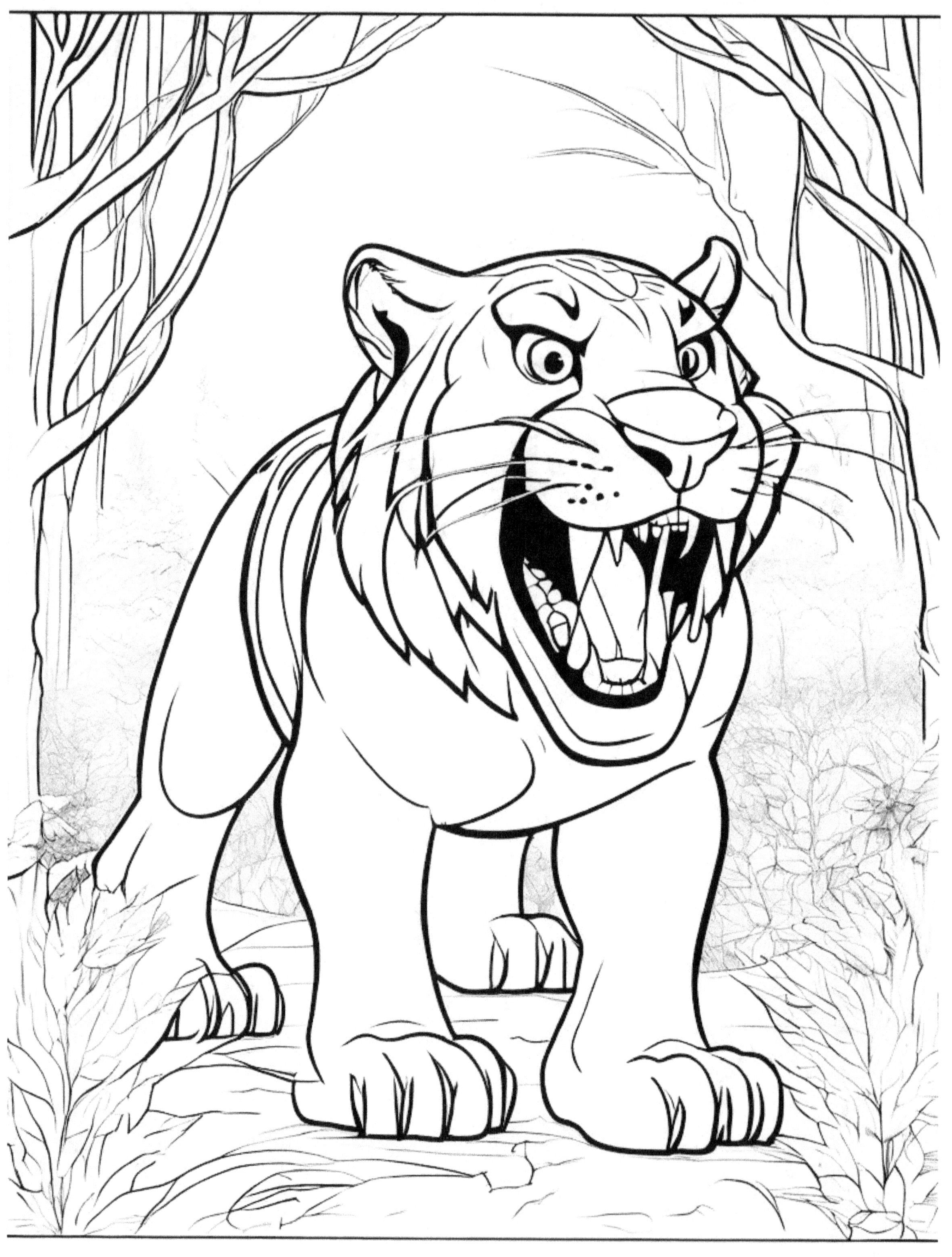

"Sabre-toothed Tiger: The Ice Age Hunter"

In a frozen era, where the Earth was a vast kingdom of ice, an extraordinary predator stood out in the icy landscapes: the Saber-toothed Tiger.
Join us on a journey across the icy wastes to uncover the secrets of this formidable Ice Age hunter!

The Majesty of the Saber-Toothed Tiger: Imagine a feline of imposing size, with long, sharp fangs that jutted out like sabers, ready to cut through the freezing cold. The Saber-toothed Tiger was truly a symbol of majesty and danger in the icy tundra.

Hunting Habits and Powerful Prey: The saber-toothed tiger was a skilled hunter, specializing in ambushing its prey. Their elongated tusks were adapted for piercing the flesh of prey, including mammoths, bison and other animals of the time. These felines were true masters of hunting in the glacial landscape.

Adaptation to Cold Climate: To face the adverse conditions of the Ice Age, the Saber-toothed Tiger had a dense and thick coat, providing insulation against the intense cold. Their ability to adapt to such hostile environments is a testament to their resilience and survival skills.

Places Where It Hunted: Fossils of the Saber-toothed Tiger have been found in various parts of the world, from North America to Europe and Asia.
These cats hunted in a variety of environments, from the vast steppes to the boreal forests of the Ice Age.

The Ice Age: Exploring the era of the Saber-toothed Tiger, we are transported to a world covered in ice, where life struggled to survive.
survive in extreme conditions. Envision these majestic felines roaming the vast expanses of frozen land, hunting in the shadows of the polar night.

Icy Tundra Adventure: Intrepid adventurers, join us on this journey across the icy tundra! Imagine the vast white plains, where the Saber-toothed Tiger reigned as the ruler of the night. Come with us to explore the mysteries and wonders of this impressive Ice Age predator, a true legend of ages past!

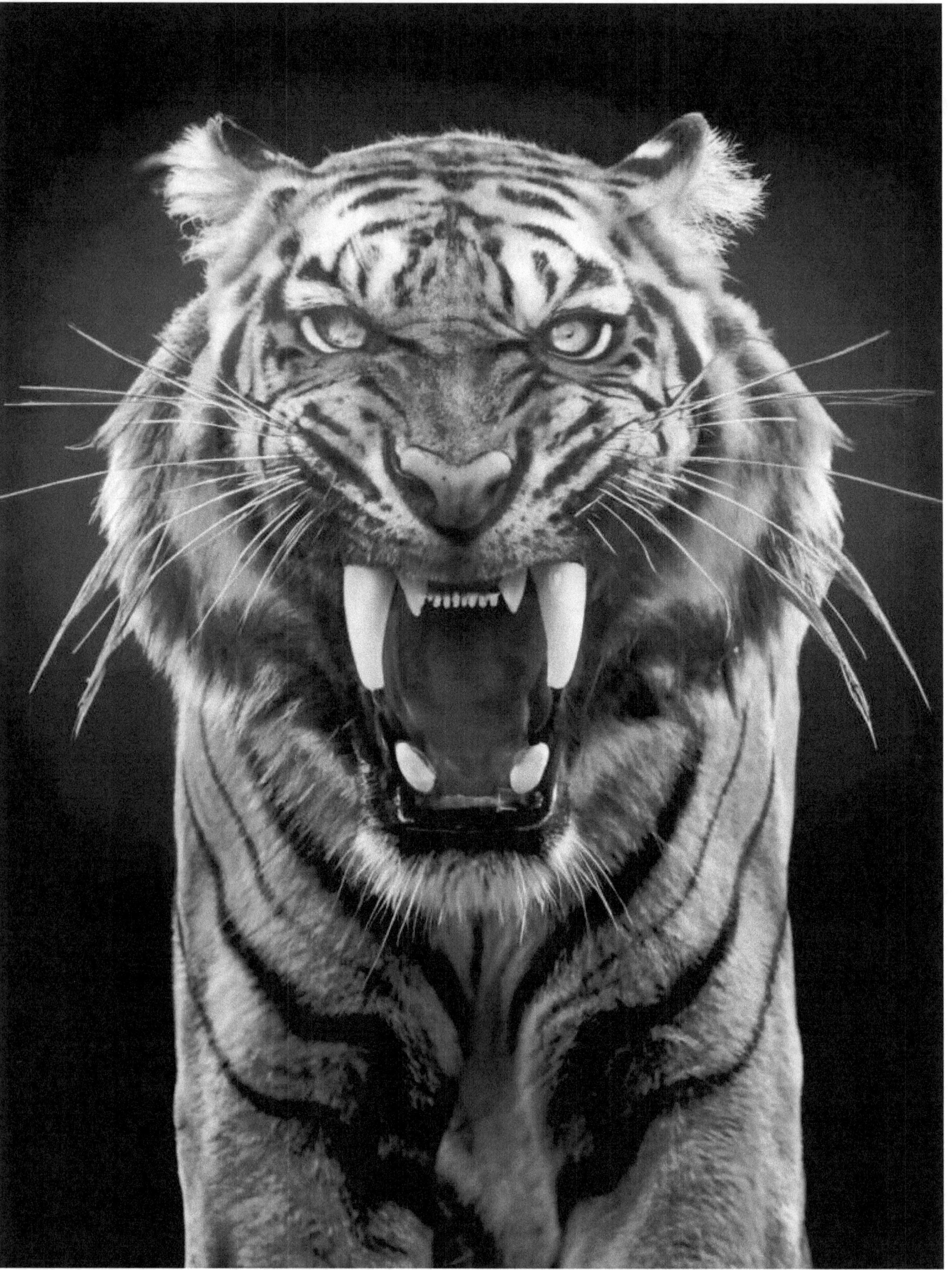

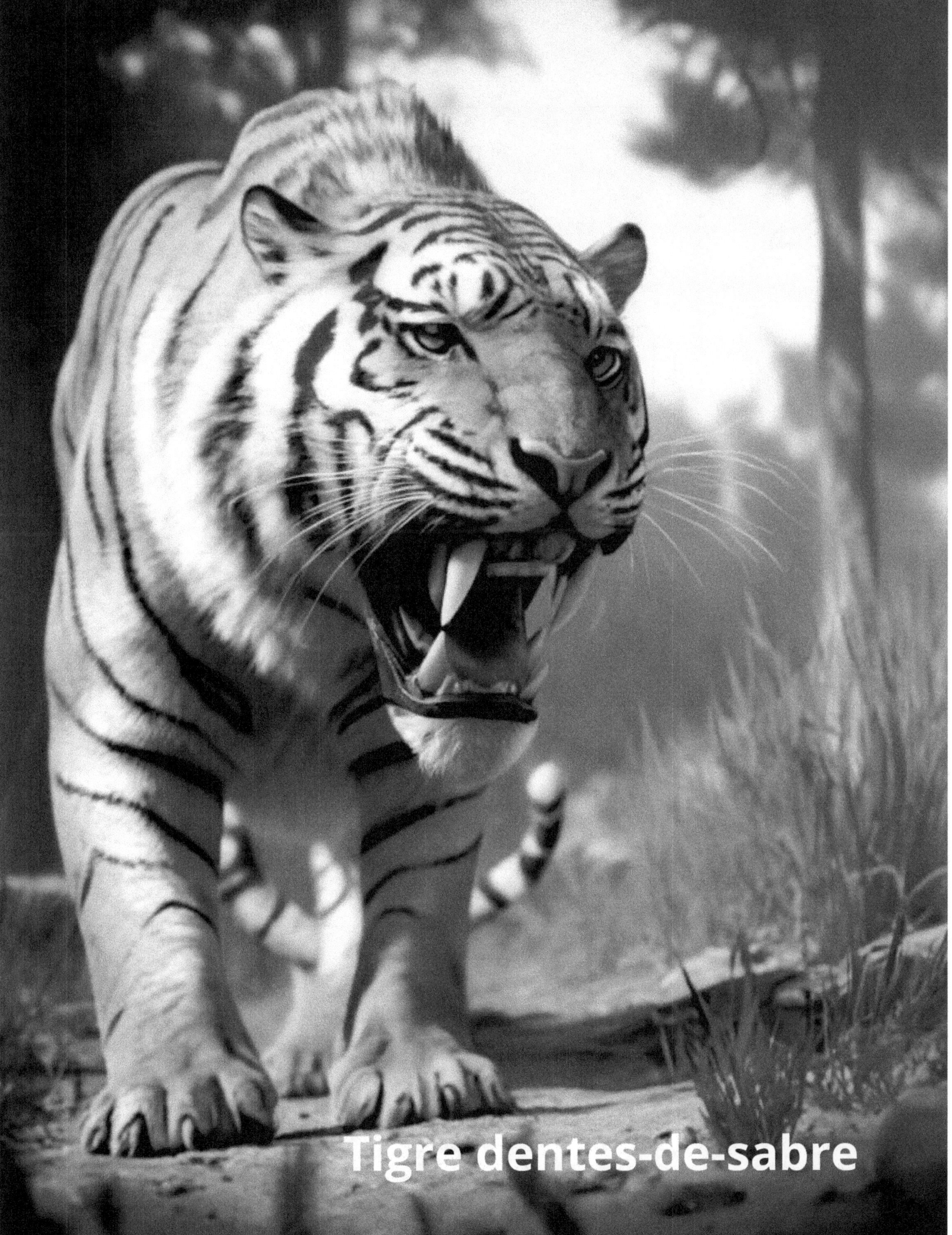
Tigre dentes-de-sabre

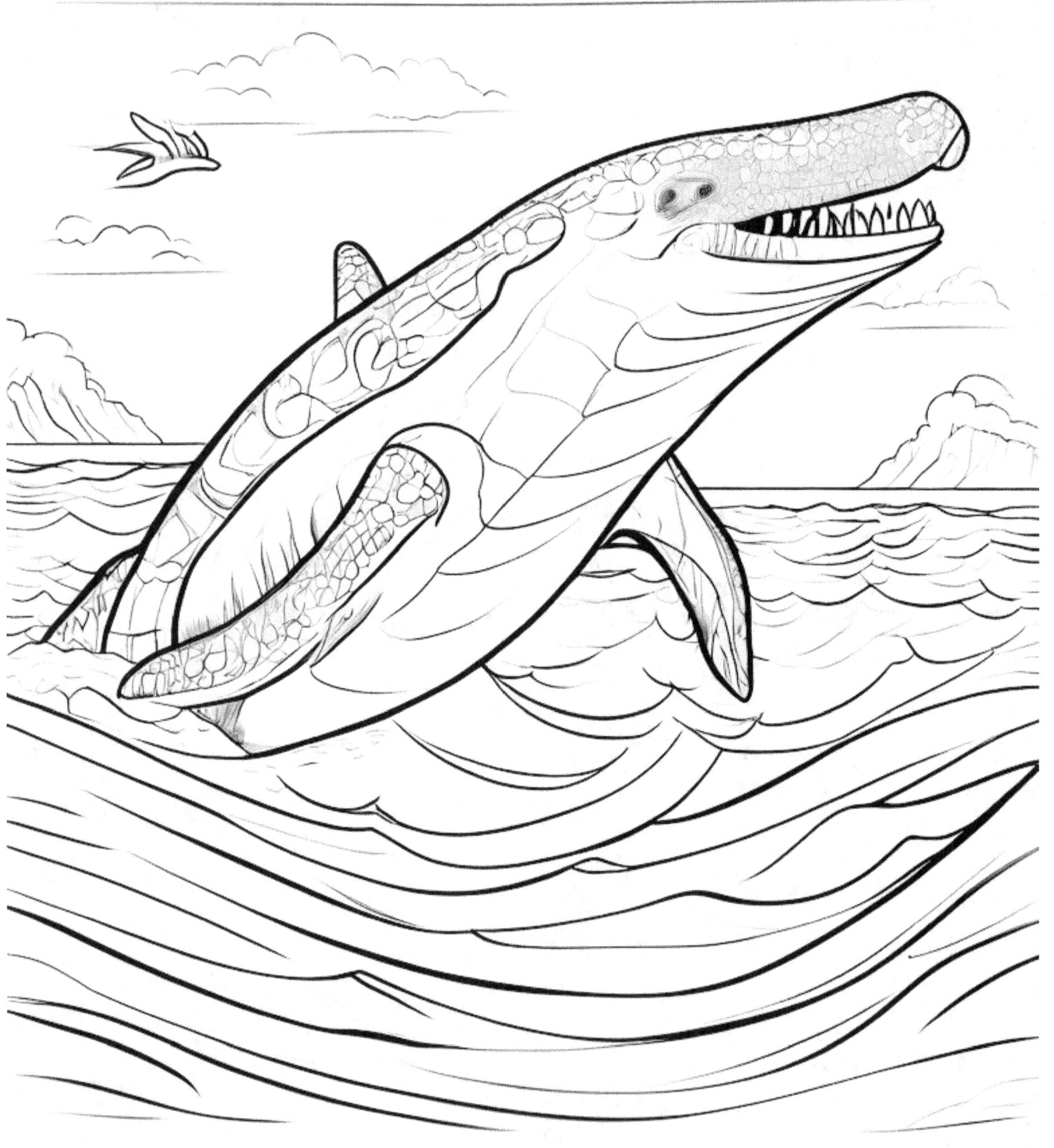

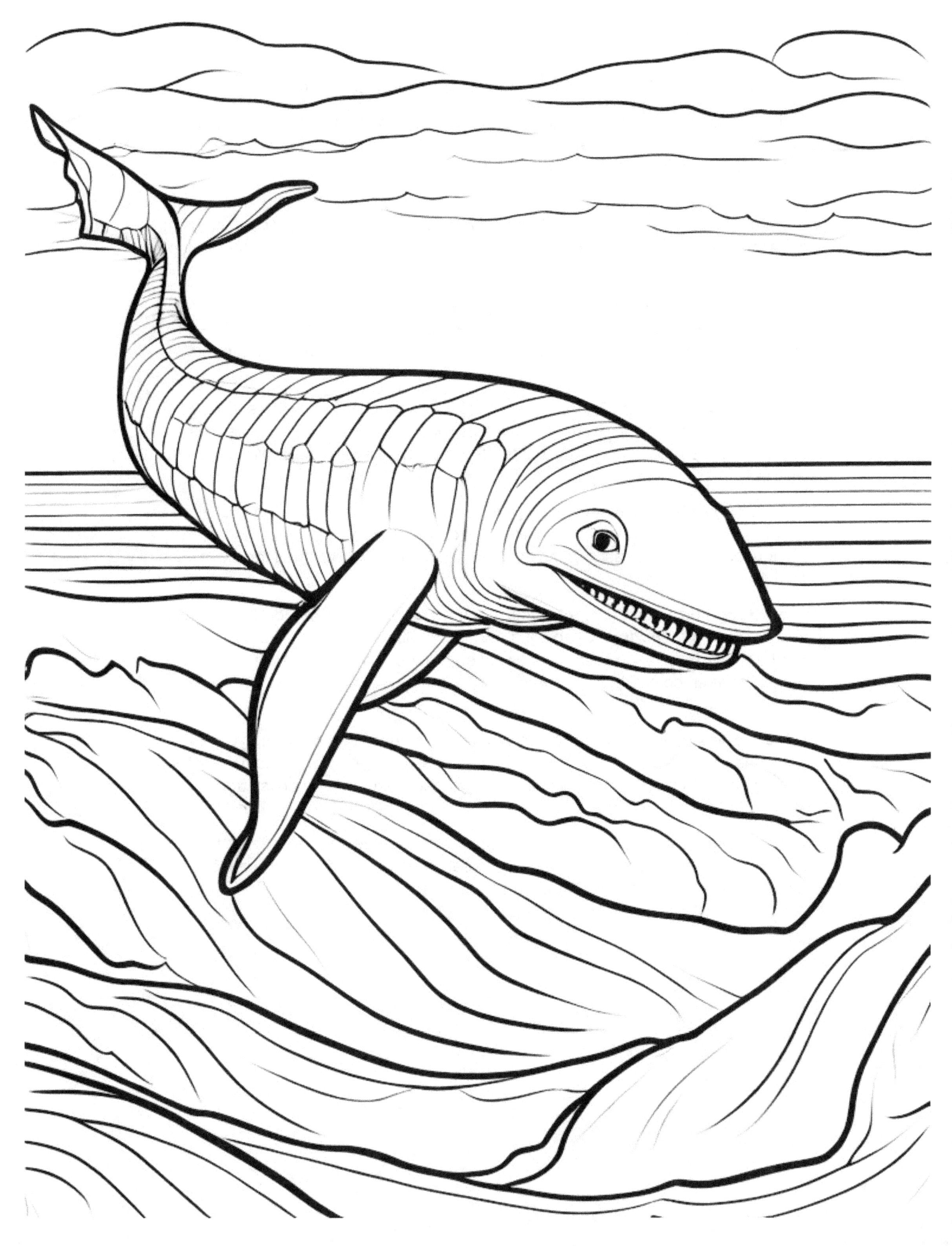

Title: "Sperm Whale: The Deep Mysteries of the Ocean Giant"

In the blue and mysterious vastness of the oceans, a giant of the depths rules the waters: the Sperm Whale. Let's dive into the depths of the ocean to discover the secrets and wonders of this magnificent cetacean.

The Magnificence of the Sperm Whale: Imagine a whale with a huge head, powerful jaws and a distinctive tail. The Sperm Whale is truly magnificent, standing out as the greatest predator in the oceans and a master of the underwater depths.

Hunting Habits and Powerful Diet: The Sperm Whale is known for its incredible hunting abilities, feeding mainly on giant squid and other marine animals. Their jaws are adapted for hunting in the dark depths, where their prey can be found in abundance.

Life in the Deep Ocean: These majestic creatures inhabit deep waters around the world, diving to great depths in search of food. Its ability to explore the most remote regions of the oceans makes the Sperm Whale a fearless explorer of dark waters.

Places Where Sperm Whales Navigate: Sperm whales can be found in all oceans, from the icy waters of the Arctic to tropical regions.
Their migrations span vast distances, crossing the seas in search of food and companionship.

Deep Song and Social Communities: Sperm whales are known for their complex vocalizations, producing a "deep song" that resonates across the oceans. Furthermore, they live in social groups called "bando" or "escol", forming lasting bonds between community members.

Underwater Adventure with Sperm Whales: Adventurous kids, close your eyes and imagine diving into the depths of the ocean alongside Sperm Whales. Envision these gentle giants swimming gracefully, exploring the undersea abyss and sharing their profound songs.

Join us on this underwater journey to explore the mysteries and wonders of the Sperm Whale, the giant of the oceans, a creature whose profound presence echoes in the waters of our blue planet.

Cachalote

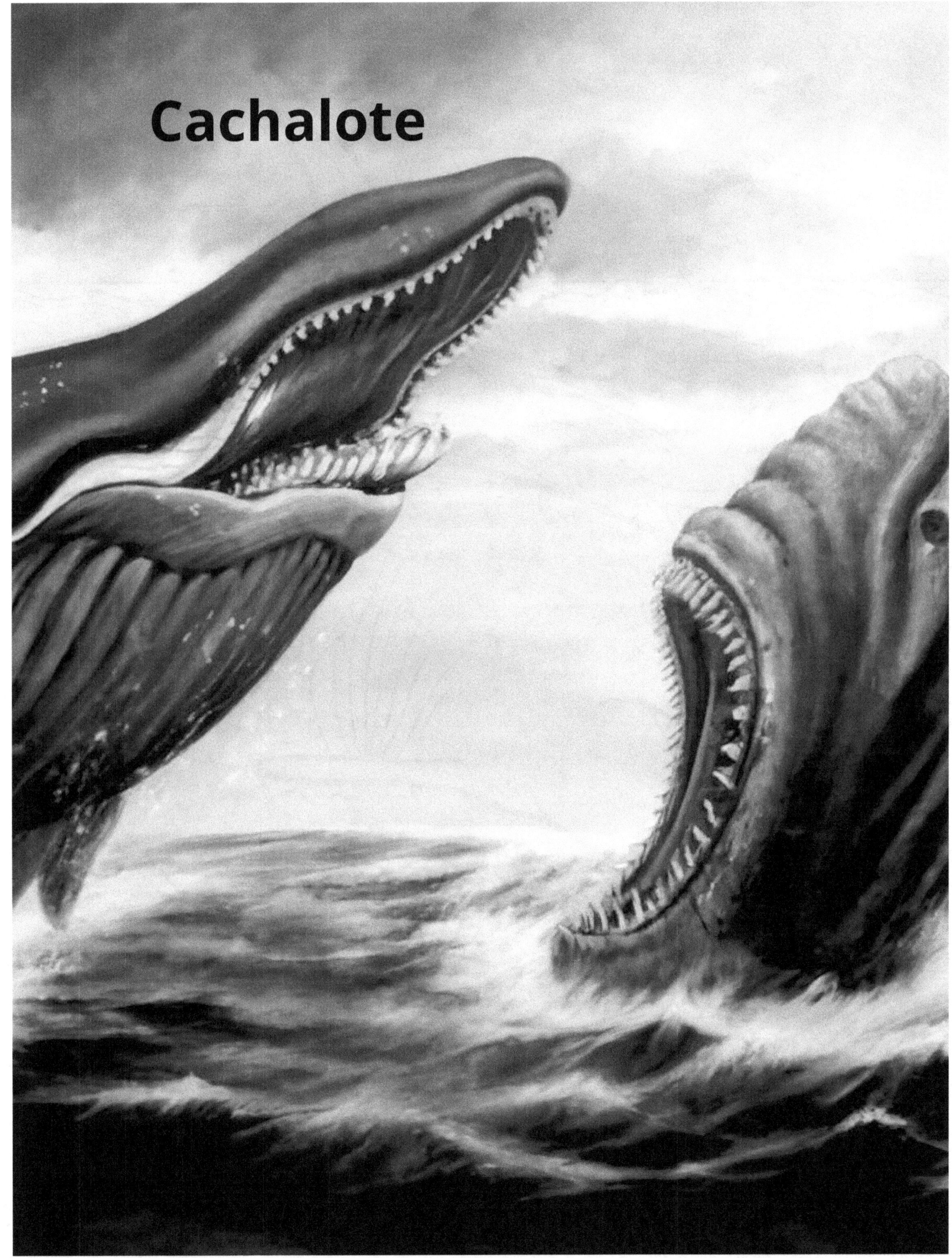

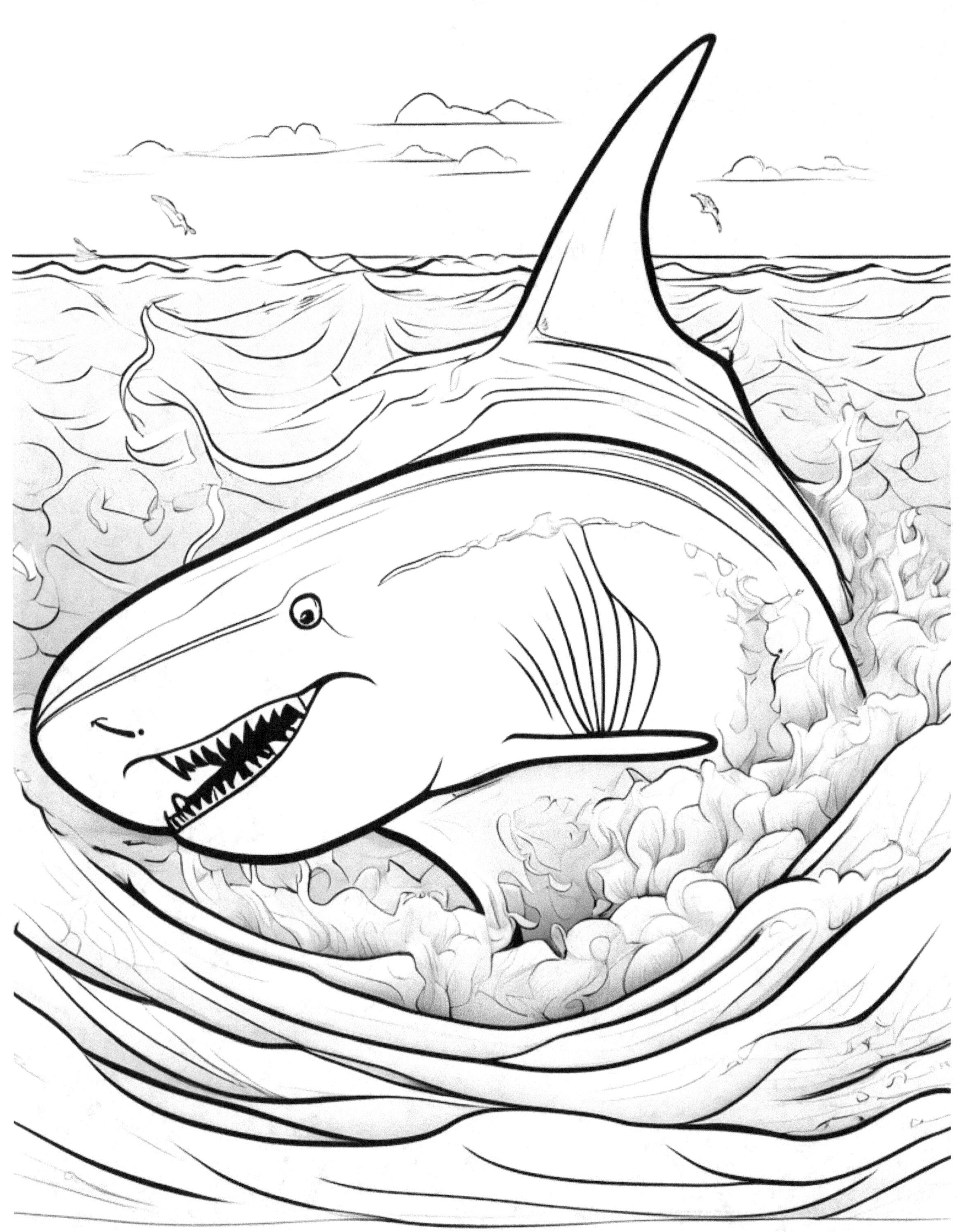

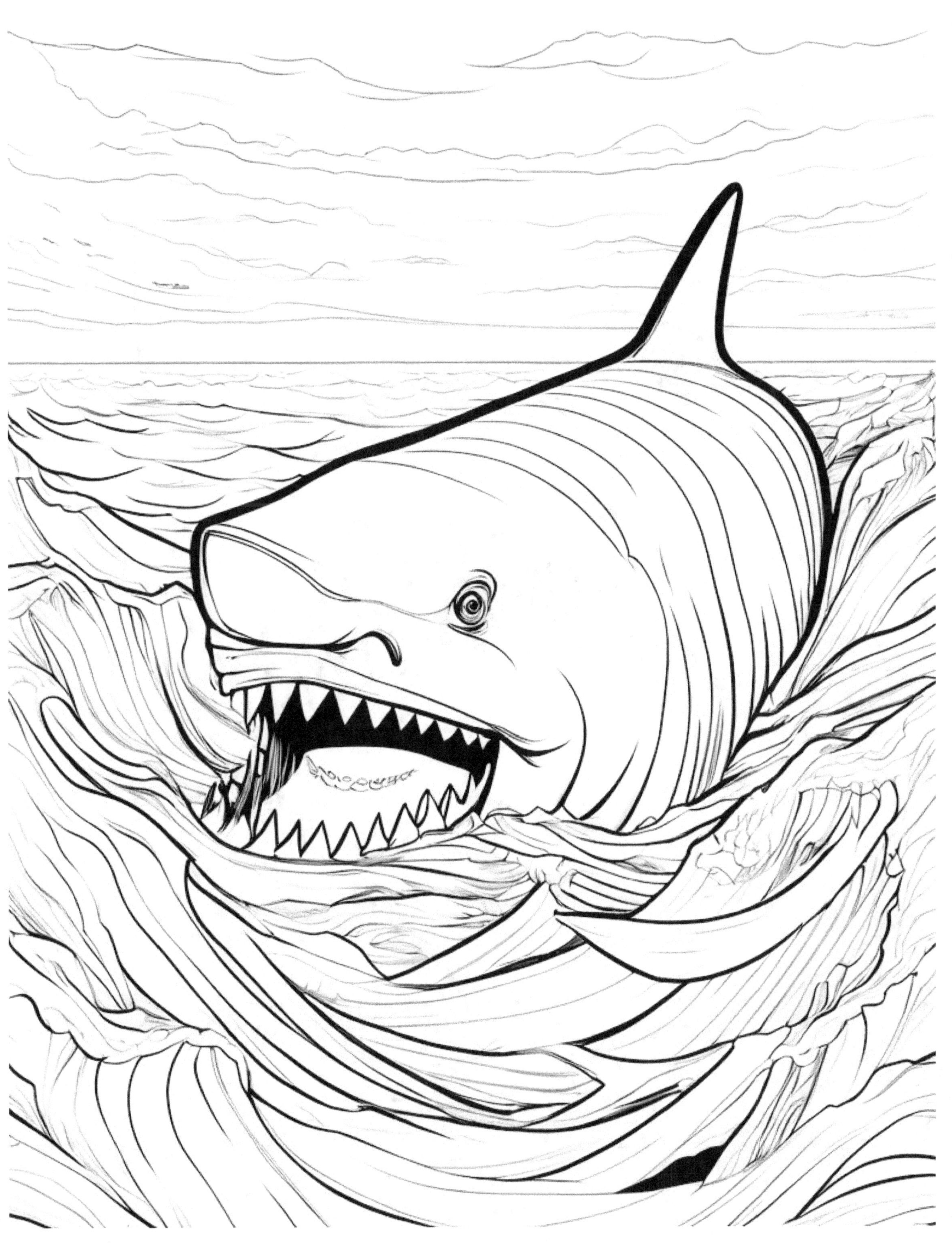

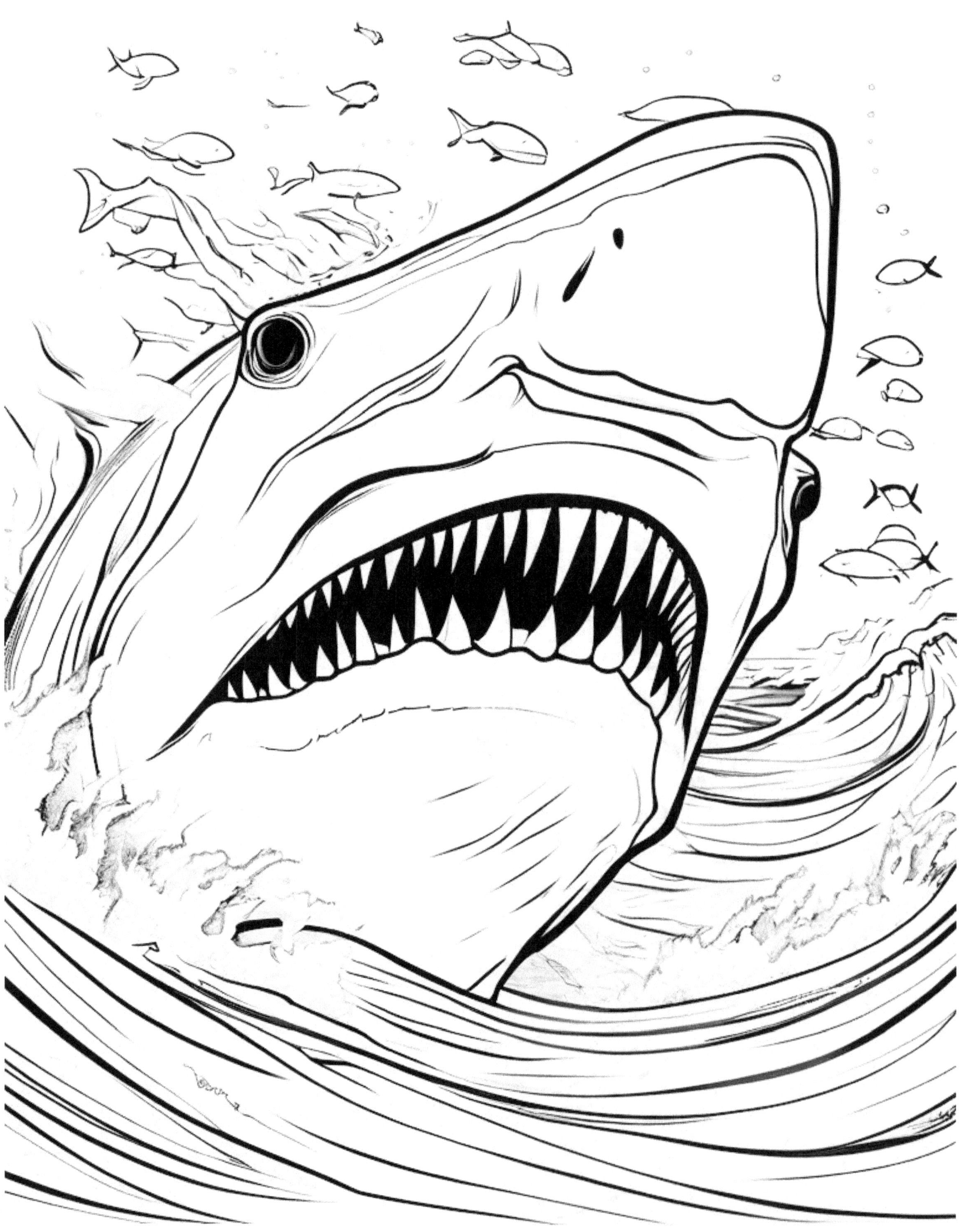

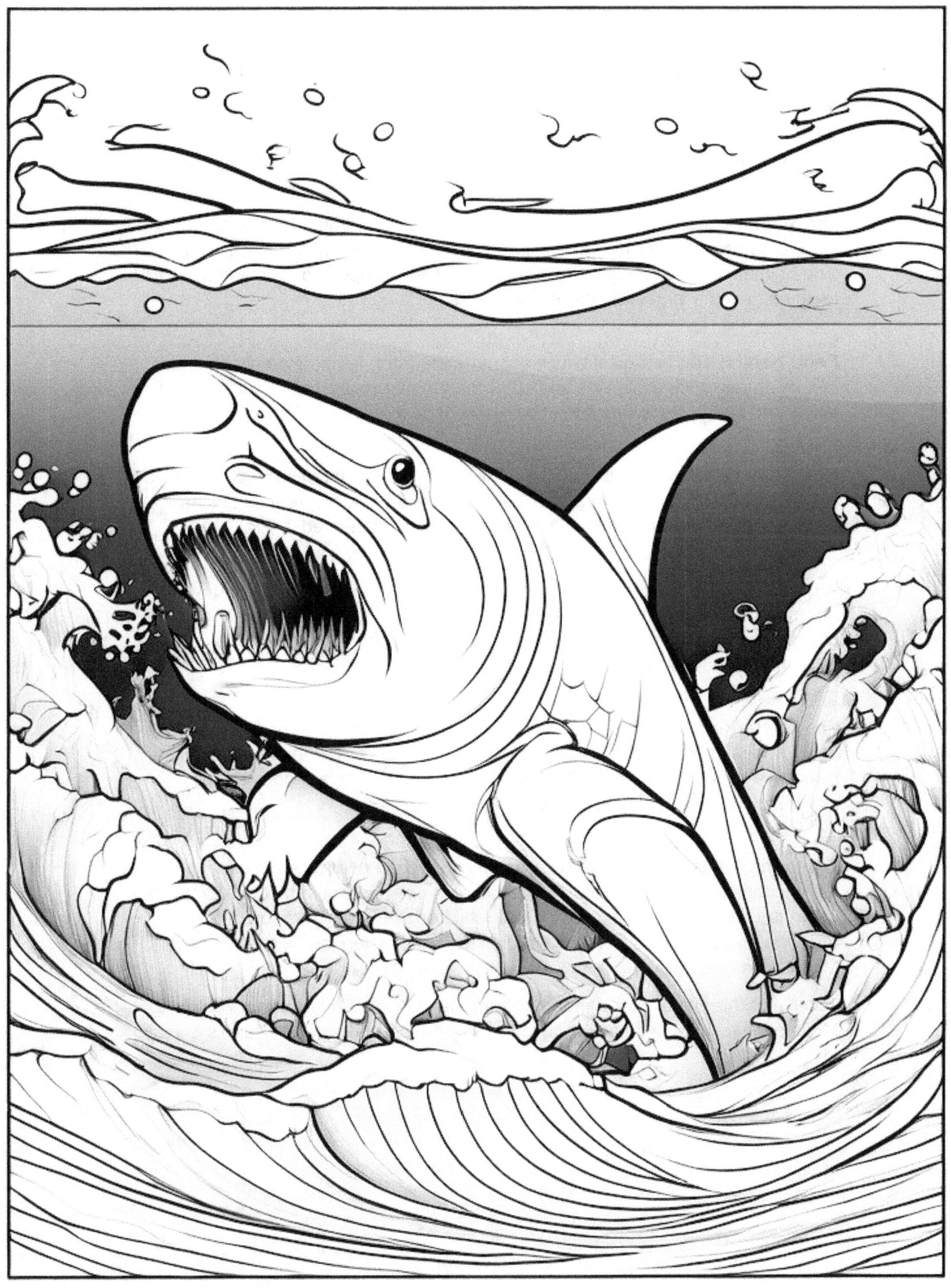

"In the Depths of the Ocean: The Mysterious Megalodon"

In a time long ago, when the oceans were vast and unexplored, a giant of the deep ruled the waters: the fearsome Megalodon.
Join us on this journey to discover the secrets of this incredible marine predator!

The Magnificence of the Megalodon: The Megalodon was a true wonder of the seas, a colossal shark that surpassed any contemporary sea creature. With lengths that could reach up to 20 meters or more, its imposing jaws and serrated teeth made it the largest predator in the oceans.

Food Habits: This sea giant was a supreme predator, feeding mainly on large sea creatures, such as whales and other marine mammals. His incredible hunting ability and speed made him a fearsome presence in ocean waters.

How They Lived: Megalodon was a perfect survival machine, adapted to the vast expanses of prehistoric oceans. It is believed that it traveled great distances in search of prey, migrating from warm to cold waters as needed.

Where They Lived: Megalodons inhabited oceans around the world, but were often associated with warmer waters. Fossils and discoveries indicate that these giants may have been found in different regions, making them true lords of the seas of the Cenozoic era.

The Mysterious Extinction: Despite its dominance of the oceans for millions of years, Megalodon eventually disappeared. The exact reason for their extinction remains a mystery, but scientists believe that climate change and changes in prey availability may have played a crucial role.

Exploring the Depths: Imagine diving into the ocean depths, encountering Megalodon in its natural habitat. What incredible stories would he have to tell about the vast, unknown oceans of old? Children, get ready for a unique underwater adventure, where we will discover the mysteries and charms of Megalodon.

Join us on this virtual expedition to explore the wonders and mysteries of Megalodon, a giant that has left its indelible mark on the pages of Earth's oceanic history.

Megalodonte

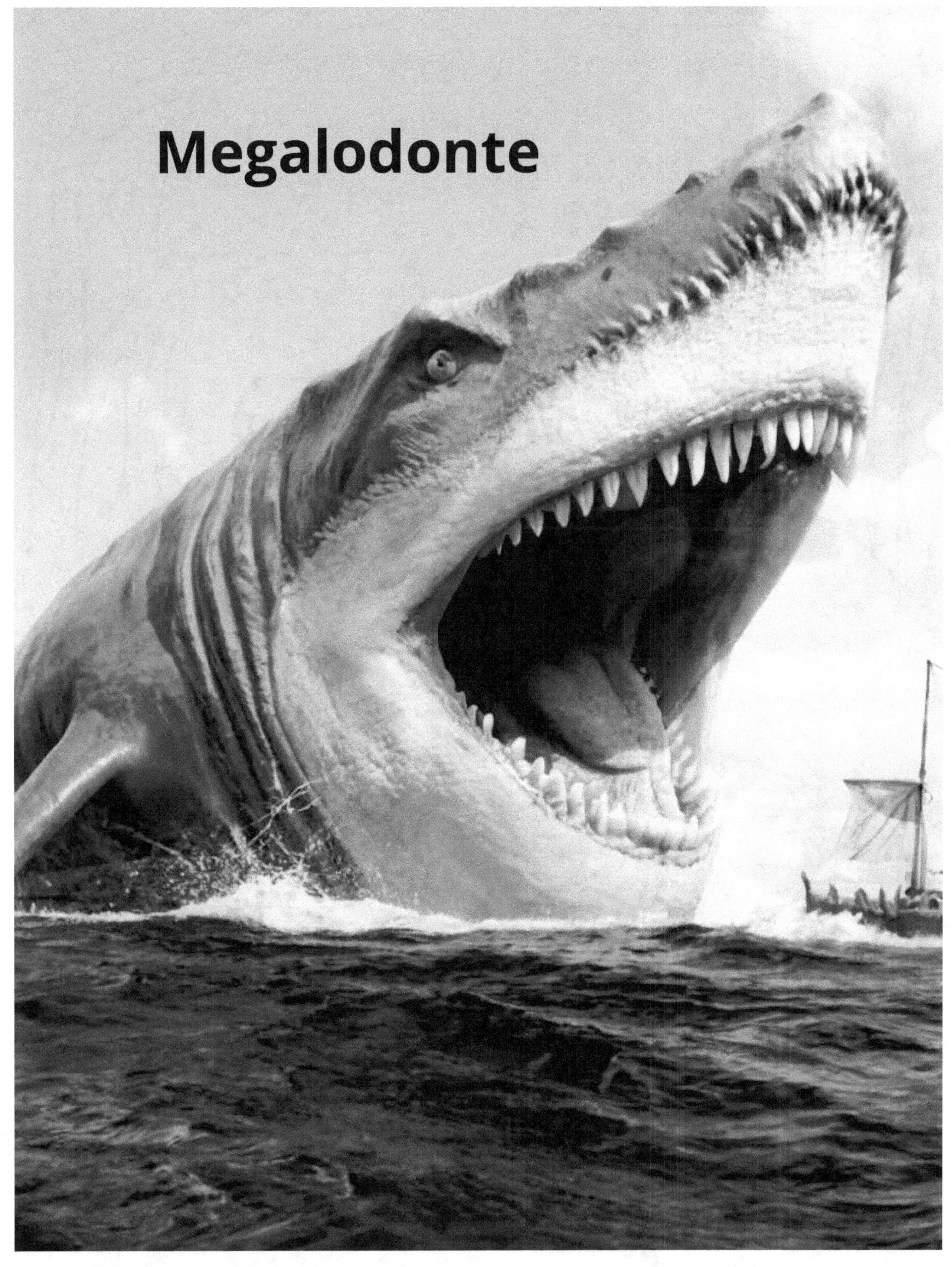

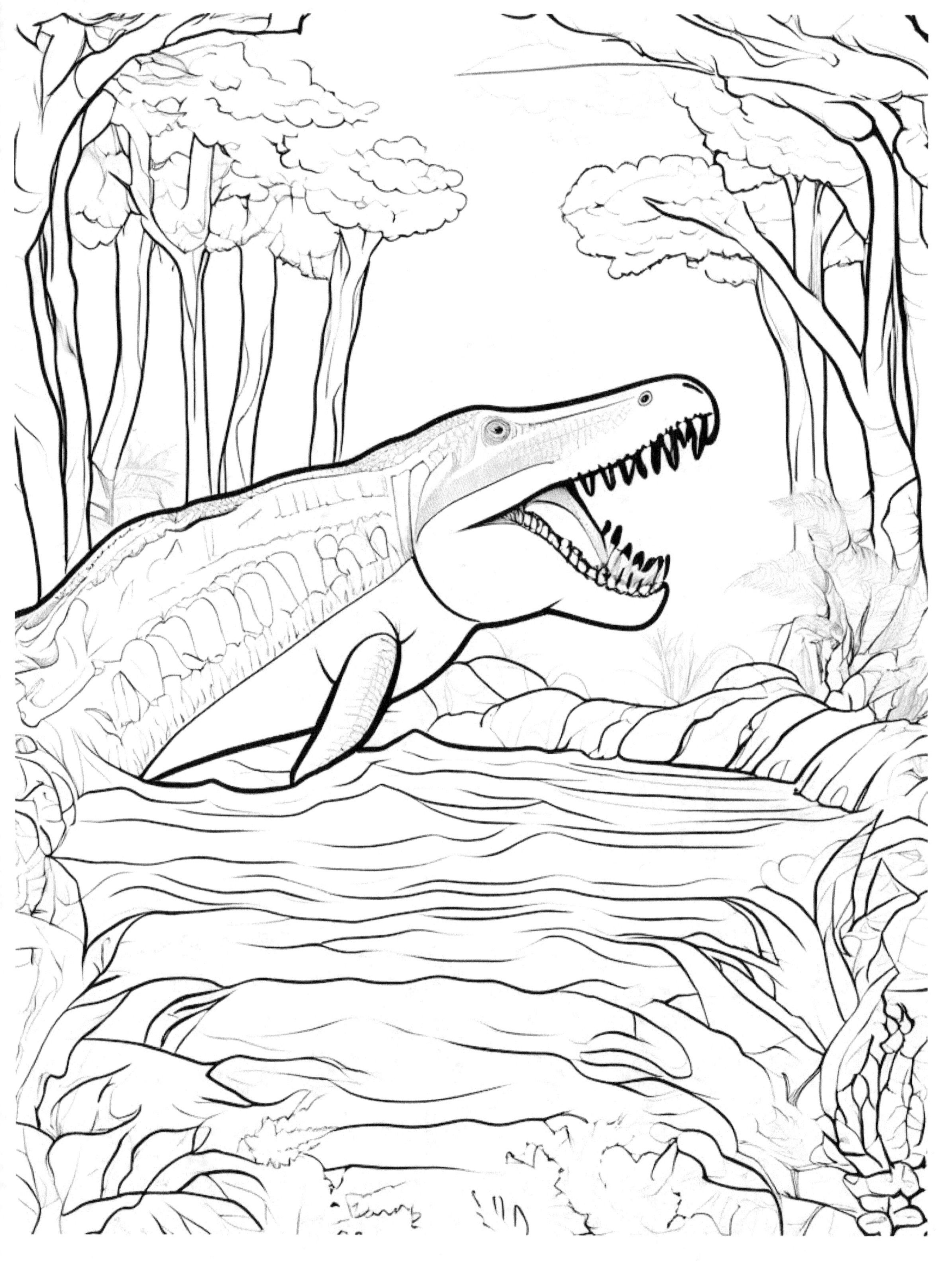

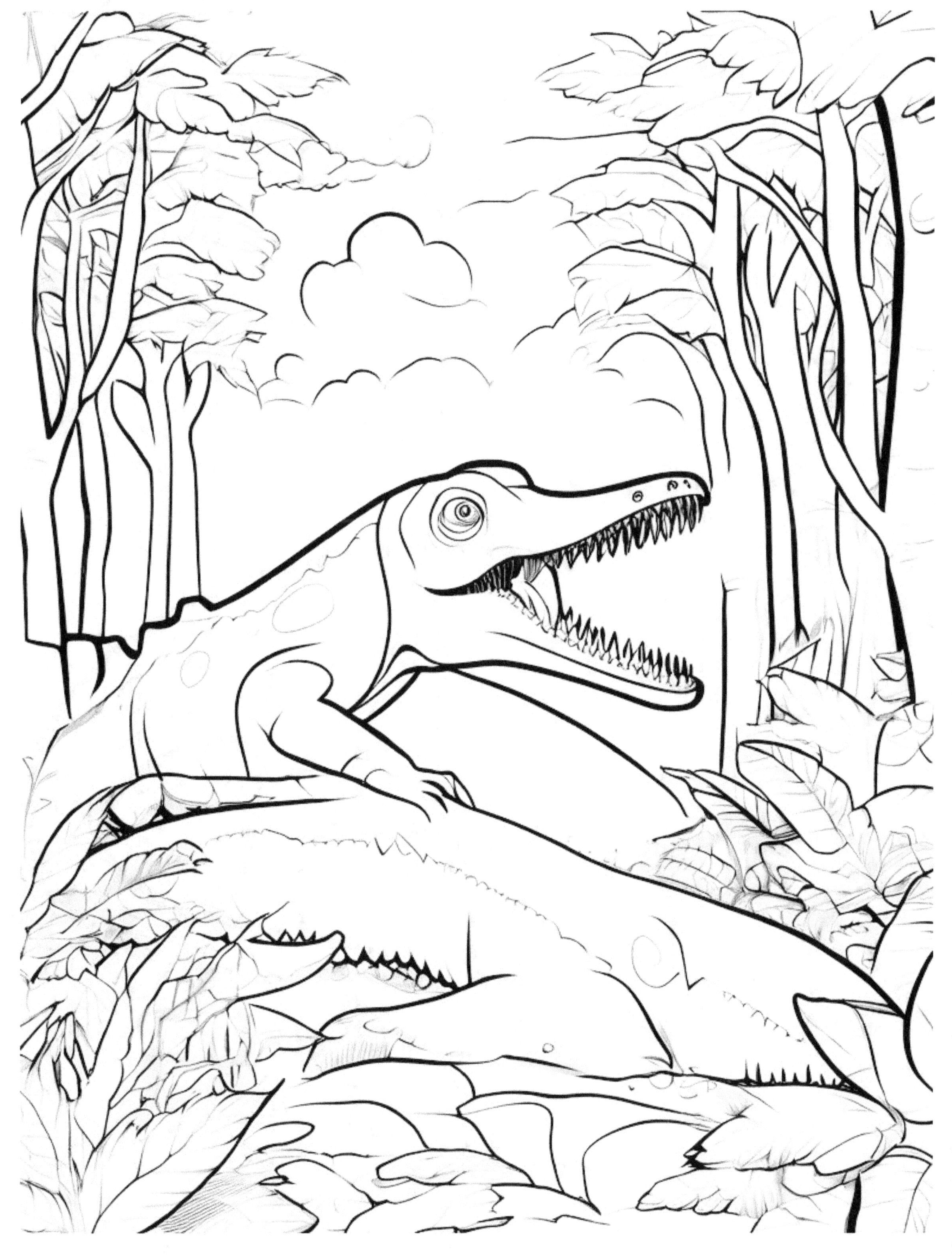

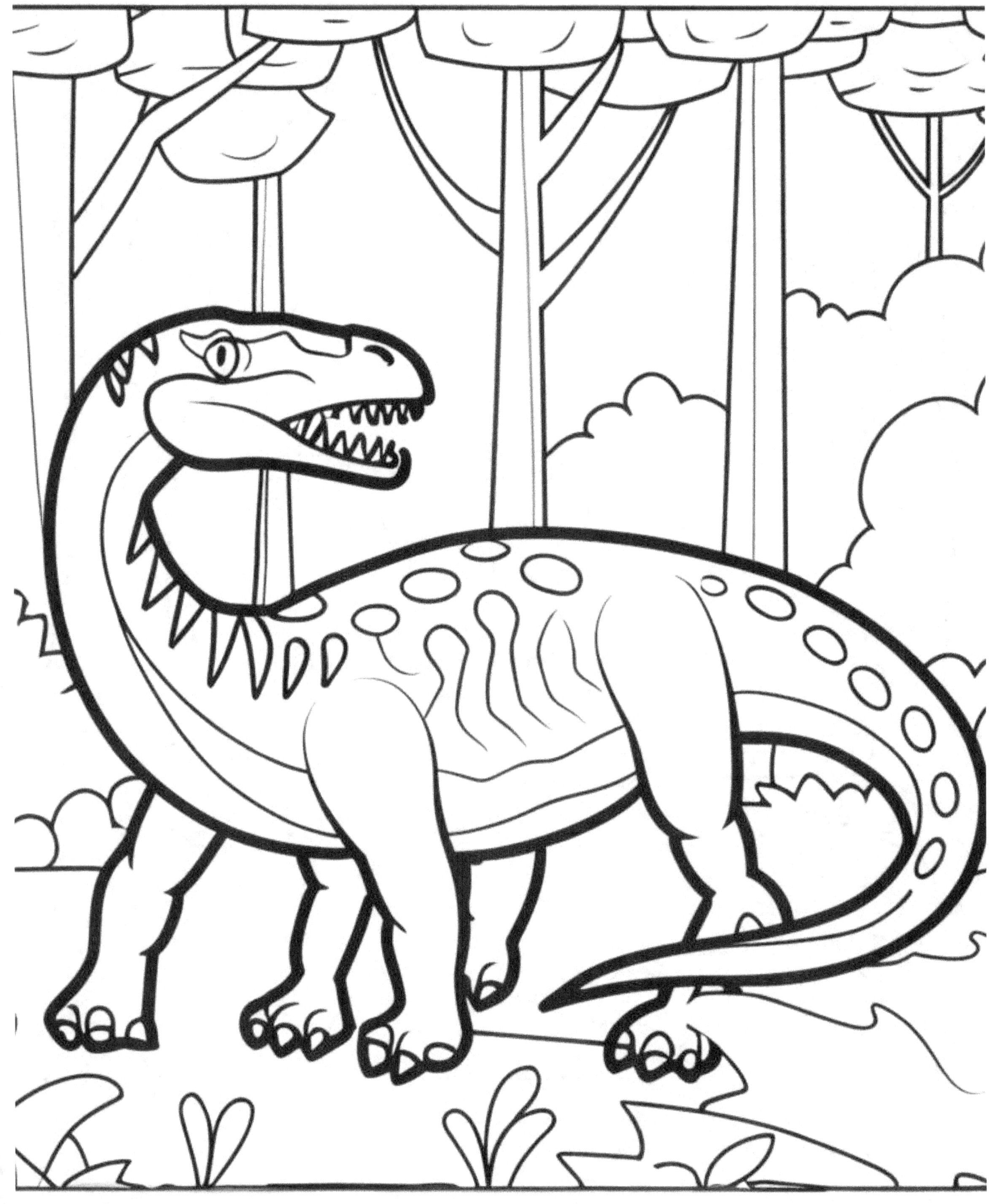

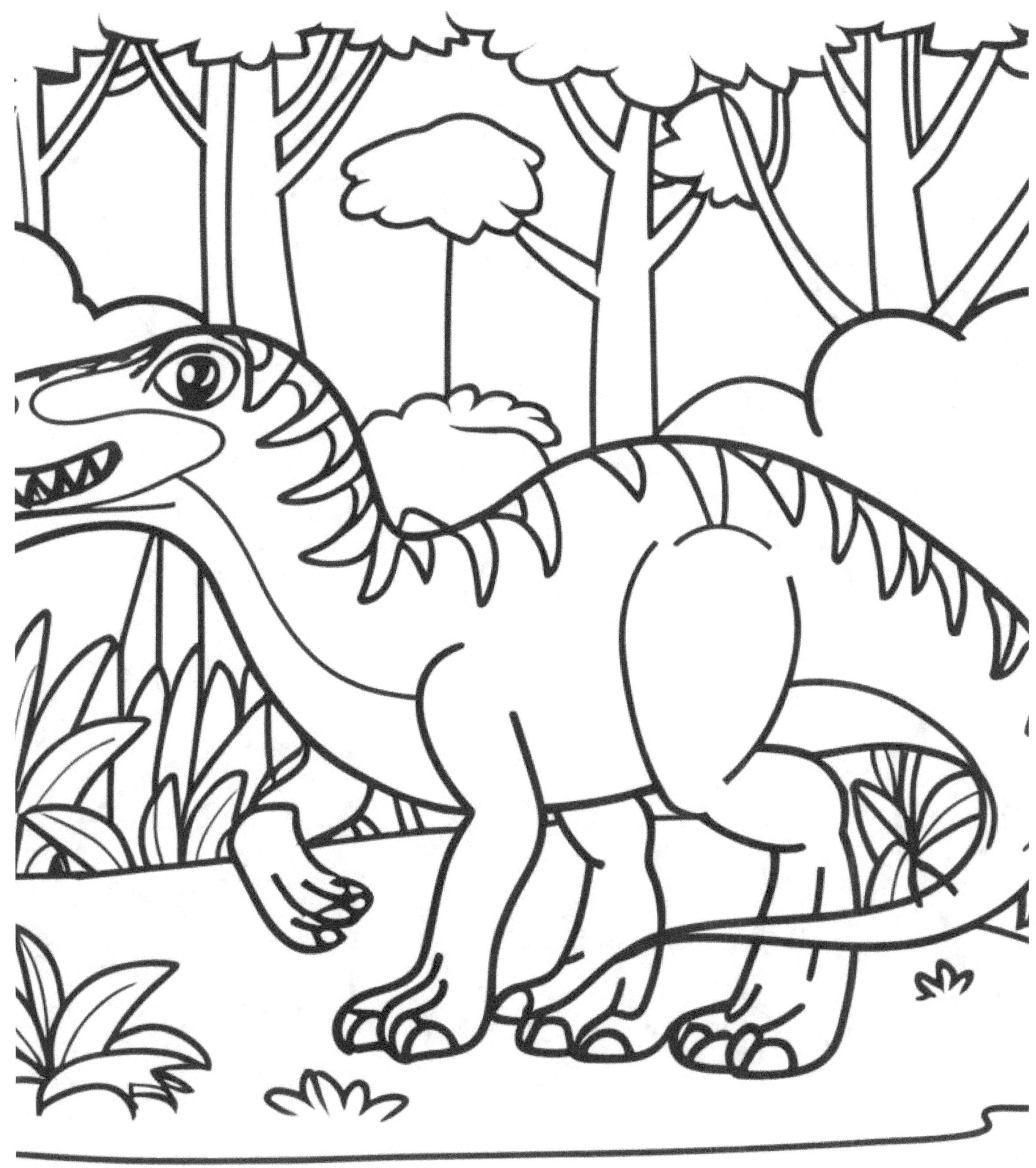

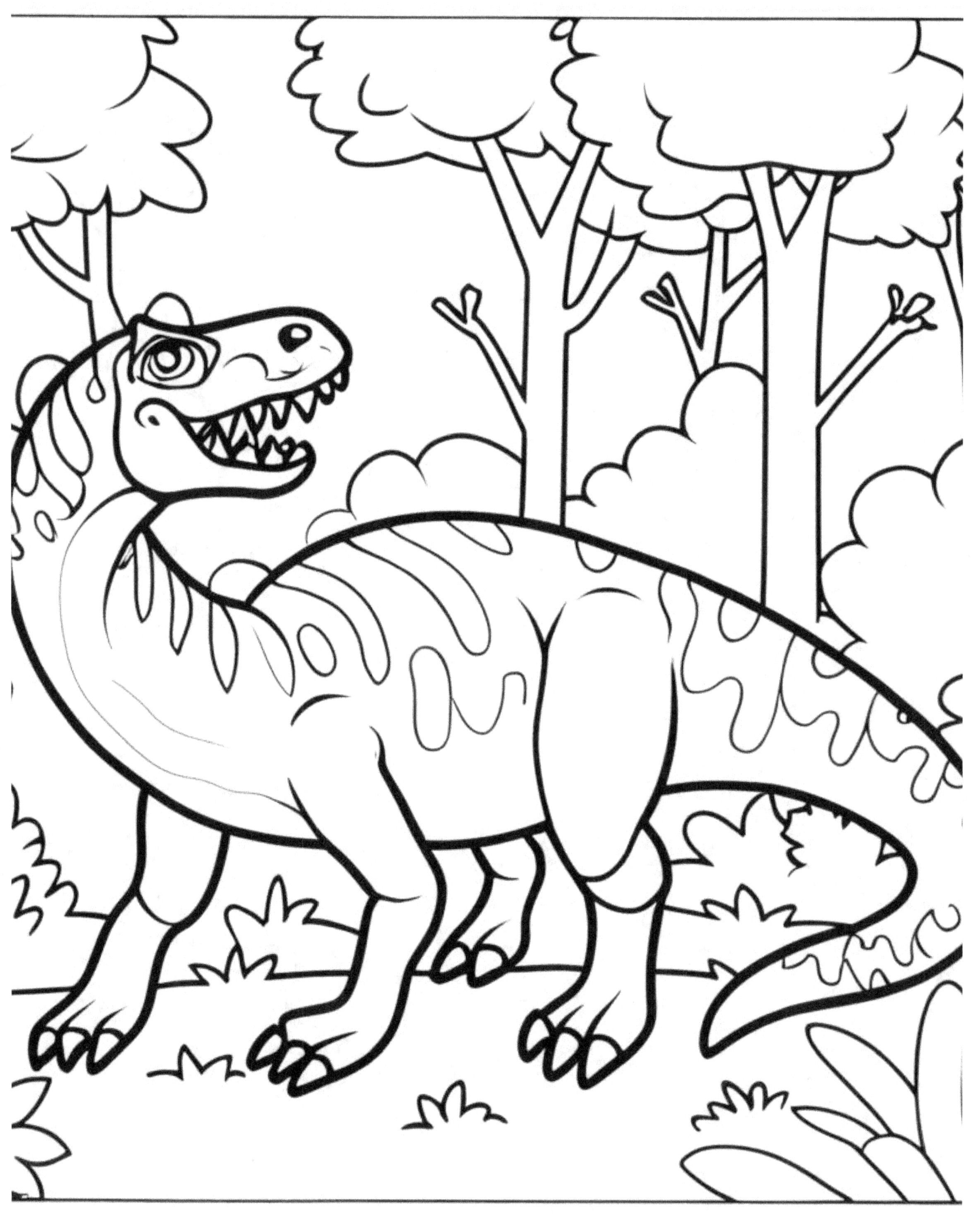

"Mosasaurus: Ruler of the Cretaceous Seas"

In a sea full of mysteries in the Cretaceous Era, a marine predator dominated the depths: the Mosasaurus. Let's embark on an underwater journey to explore the secrets of this giant of the seas!

The Magnificence of the Mosasaurus: Imagine a sea creature with an impressive head, sharp teeth and an elongated body that cut through the waters with elegance. The Mosasaurus was truly the ruler of the Cretaceous seas, displaying unique magnificence.

Food Habits and Efficient Hunting: The Mosasaurus was a voracious predator, feeding mainly on fish, ammonites, and even other marine reptiles. With sharp teeth and powerful jaws, it was an efficient hunter capable of dominating the waters in search of prey.

Adaptation to Marine Life: Unlike pliosaurs, the Mosasaurus was not a reptile that lived on the surface of the ocean, but rather an agile swimmer, adapted for life in the depths. Its fins were effective for quick maneuvers, making it one of the main marine predators of its time.

Places Where It Reigned: Mosasaurus fossils have been found in numerous locations around the world, indicating that these marine predators were global inhabitants of the Cretaceous oceans. Their fossil footprints tell the story of a time when the seas were ruled by these formidable creatures.

The Time of the Deep Oceans: As we explore the time of the Mosasaurs, we are transported to a world where the oceans were deep and full of life. Envision these marine predators slicing through the dark waters, creating a magnificent spectacle in the depths of the Cretaceous seas.

Underwater Adventure: Adventurous kids, dive with us on this underwater adventure! Imagine the depths of the Cretaceous oceans, where the Mosasaurus reigns majestically. Join us to explore the mysteries and wonders of Mosasaurus, ruler of the Cretaceous seas!

Mosassauro

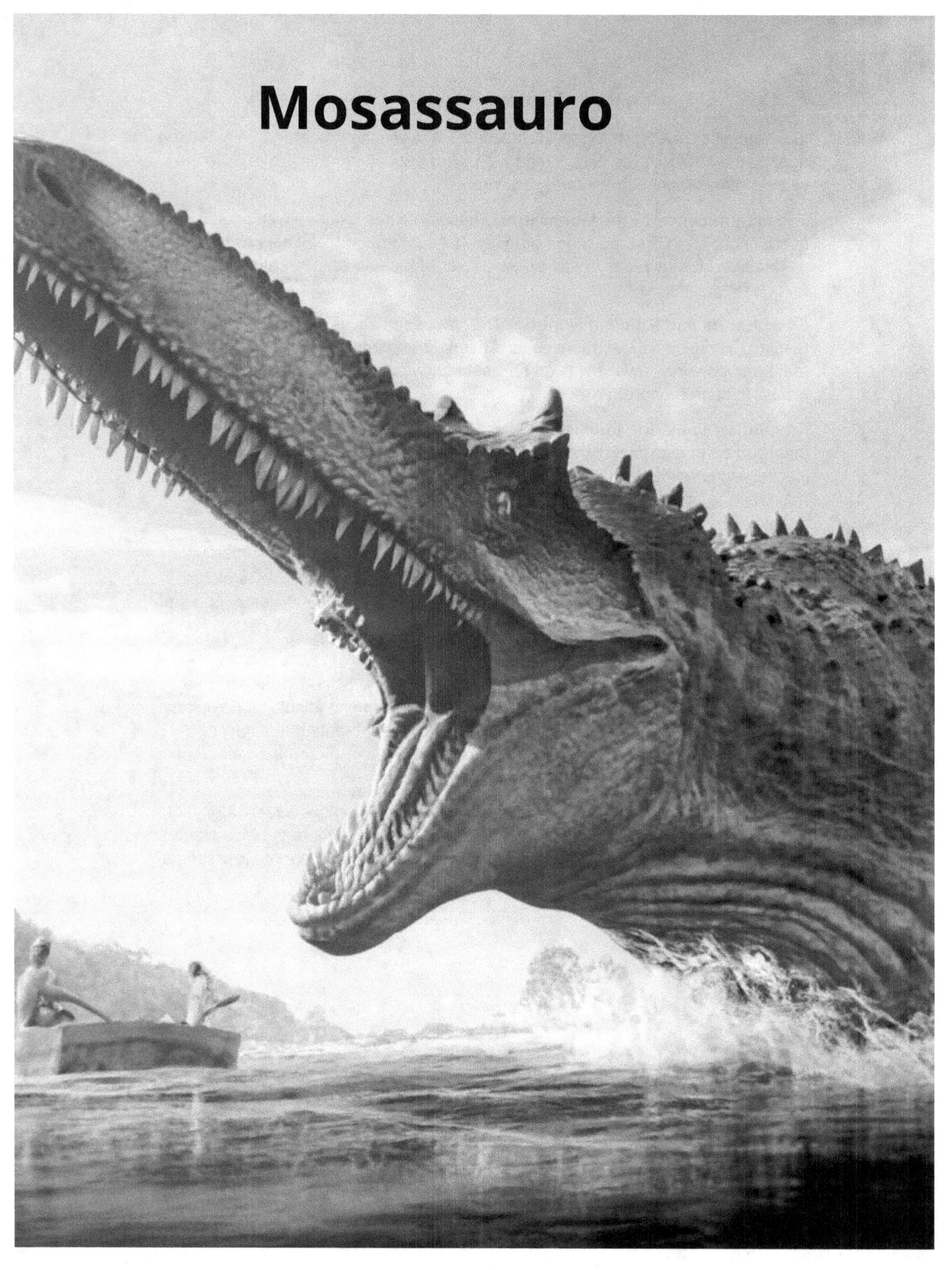

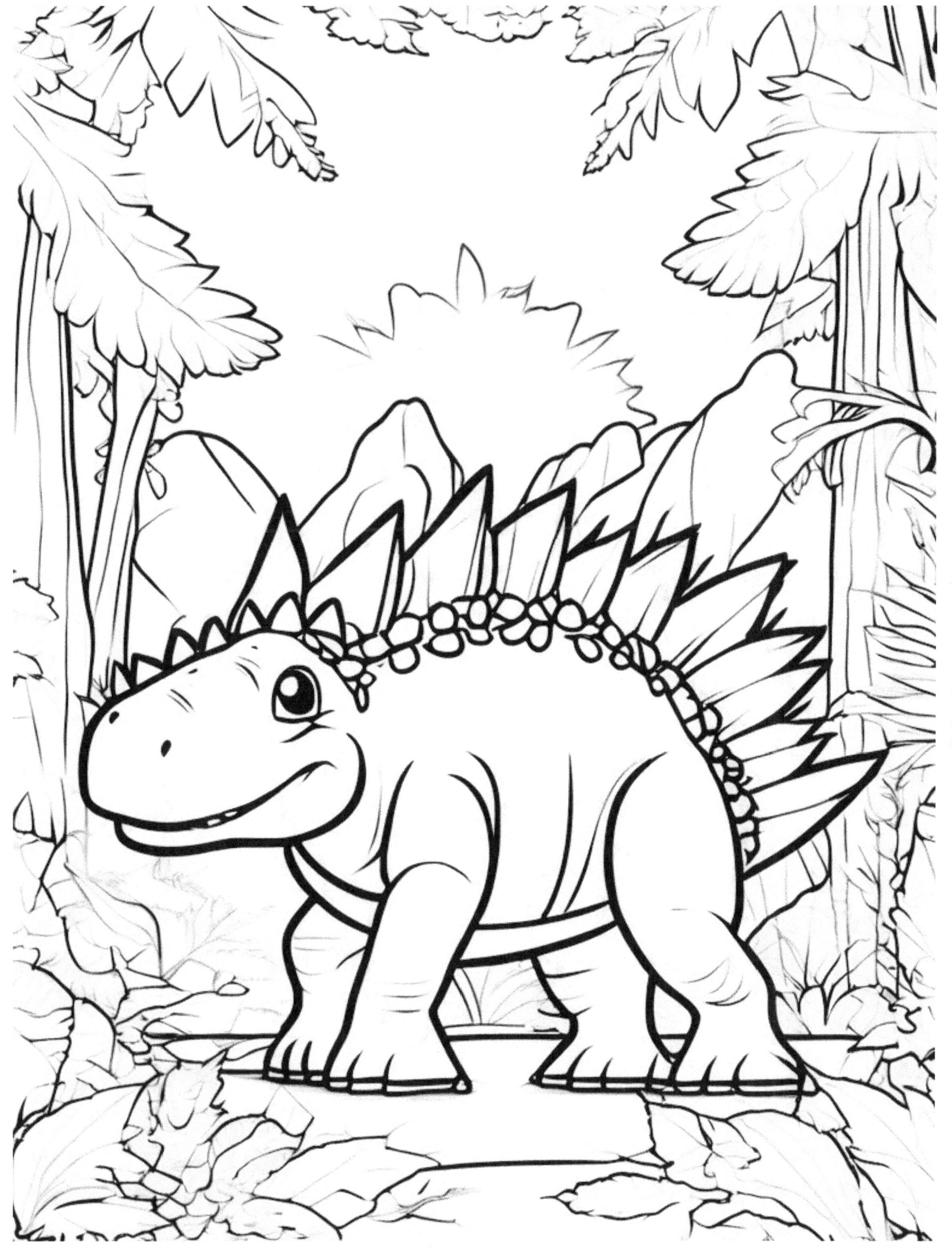

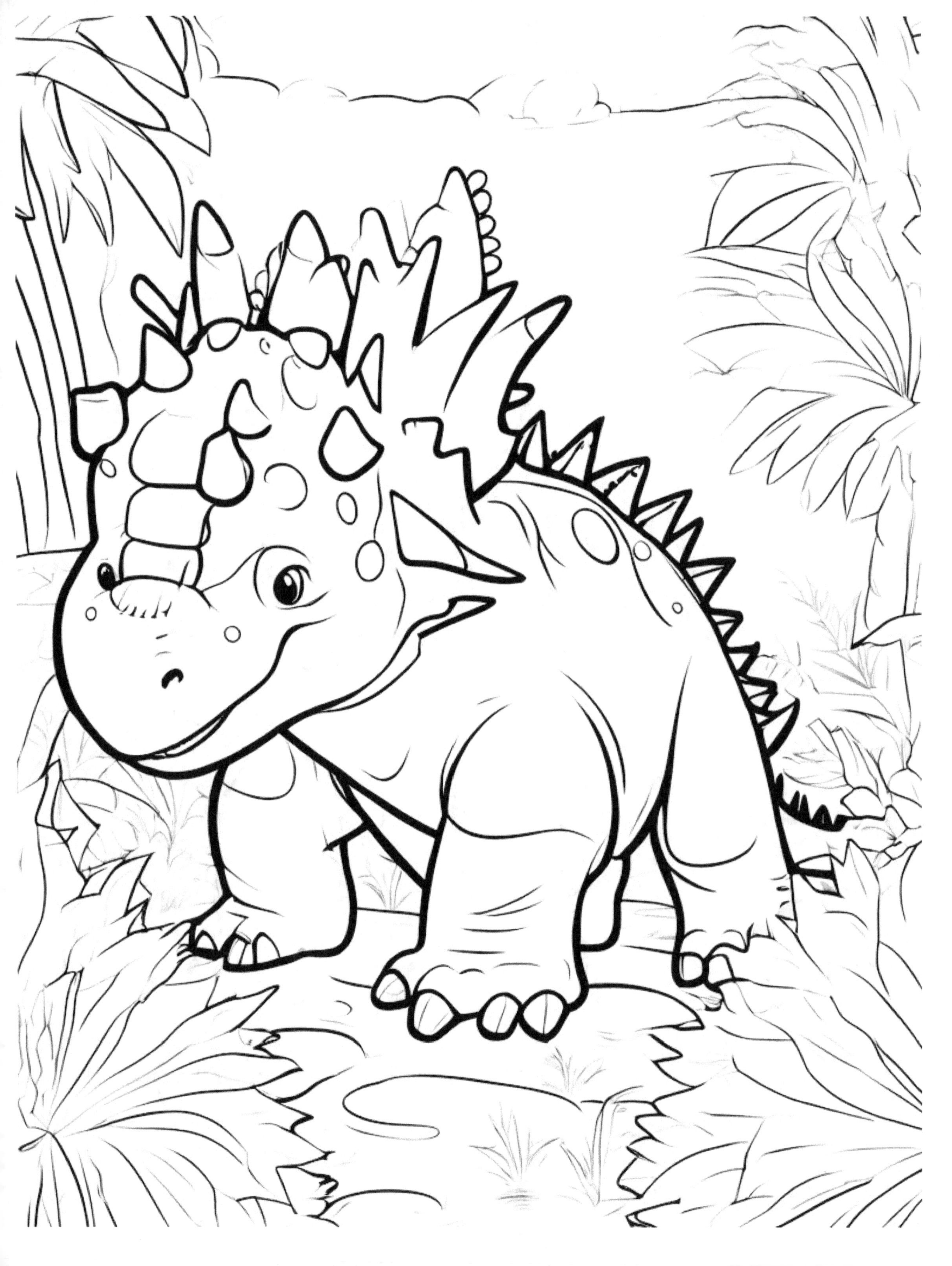

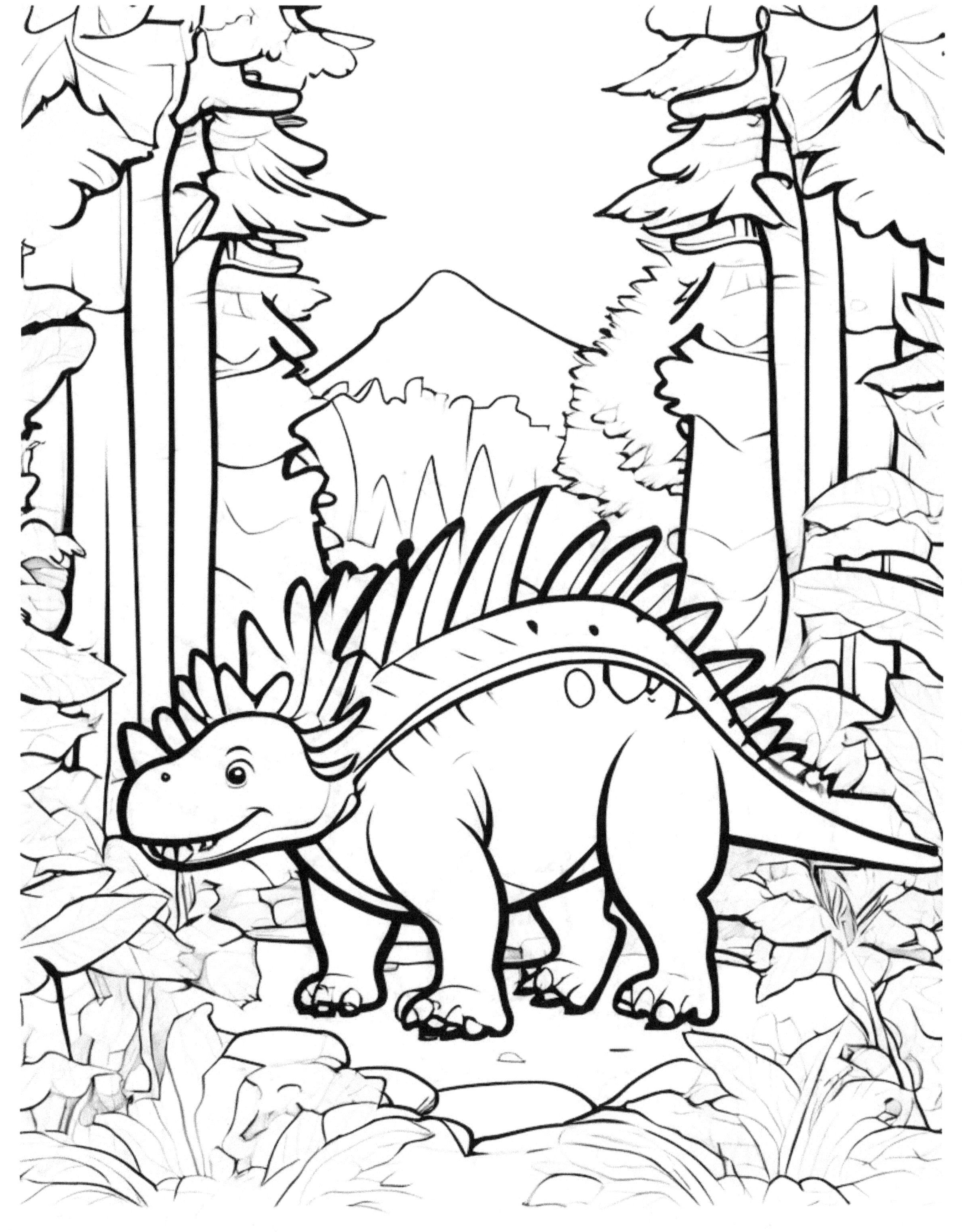

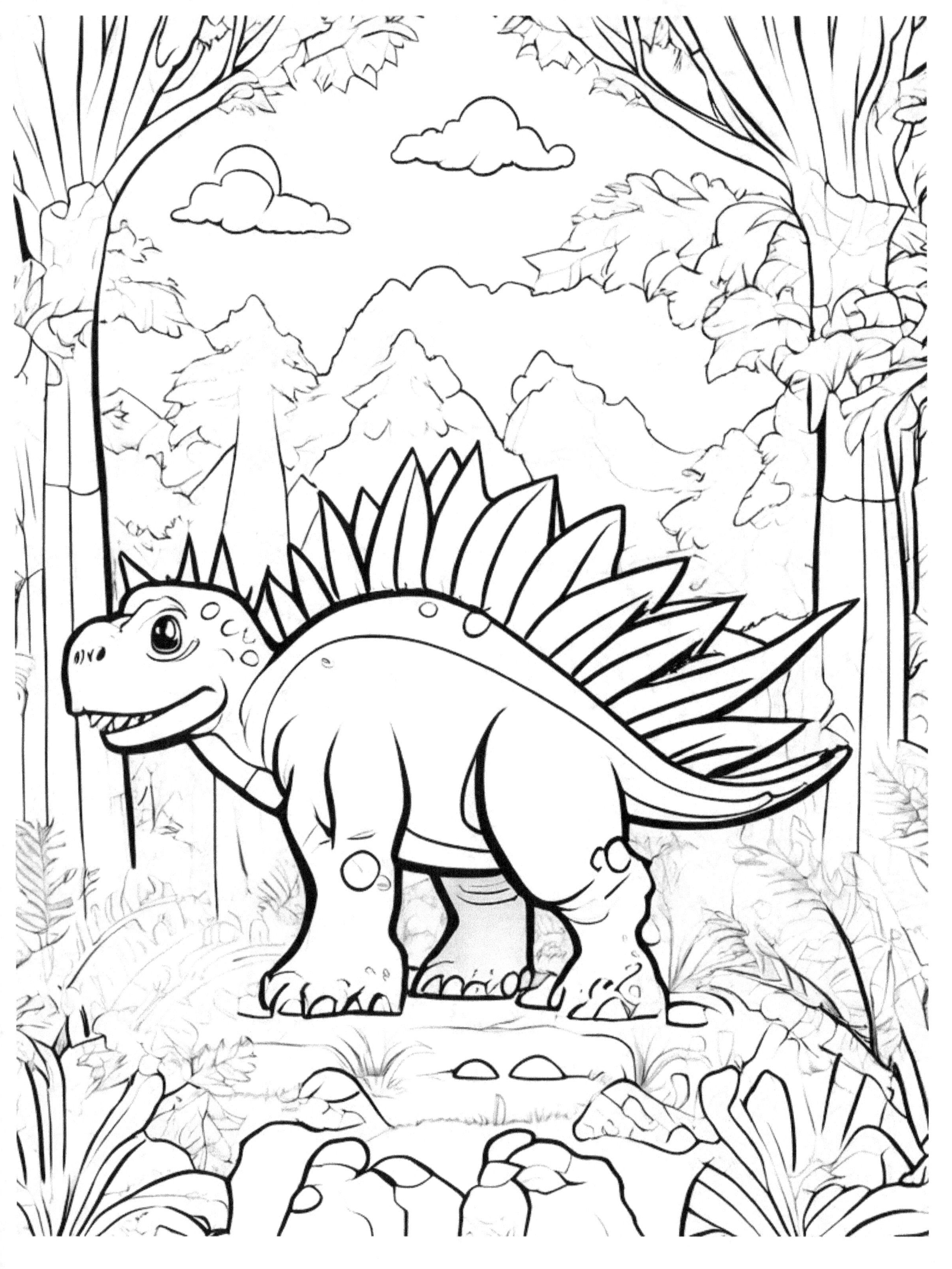

"Stegosaurus: The Thorned Guardian of the Jurassic Era"

In a world full of extraordinary dinosaurs, Stegosaurus stands out as a unique guardian of the Jurassic Era. Let's embark on an exciting journey to discover the secrets of this thorn-adorned herbivore!

The Elegance of Stegosaurus: Imagine a dinosaur with bony plates along its back, spines that project from the side and a powerful tail with sharp tips. Stegosaurus was a truly majestic creature, a herbivore that stood out for its impressive set of natural defenses.

Food Habits and Herbivory: Unlike carnivorous dinosaurs, Stegosaurus was a peaceful herbivore, feeding mainly on low plants, such as ferns and cycads. Its small head and teeth adapted for chewing indicate a diet

specialized in low-lying vegetation.

The Bone Plate Spectacle: Stegosaurus's most distinctive feature was the row of bony plates along its back. These plates functioned as a kind of natural armor, possibly
used to regulate body temperature or for display during mating rituals and social communication.

Tail Defense: In addition to the plates, Stegosaurus's tail was a formidable defensive weapon. Sharp spikes adorned the end of the tail, offering a line of defense against predators. This dinosaur could shake its tail vigorously to ward off possible threats.

How They Lived in Herds: It is believed that Stegosaurus lived in social groups called herds. Living in herds provided a collective defense against predators and the chance to share information about food sources and safe areas.

Adventures in the Jurassic World: Adventurous children, imagine walking alongside Stegosaurus in a Jurassic setting. Visualize these herbivorous dinosaurs moving gracefully among the plants, their plates and spines creating a unique spectacle in the prehistoric landscape.

Estegossauro

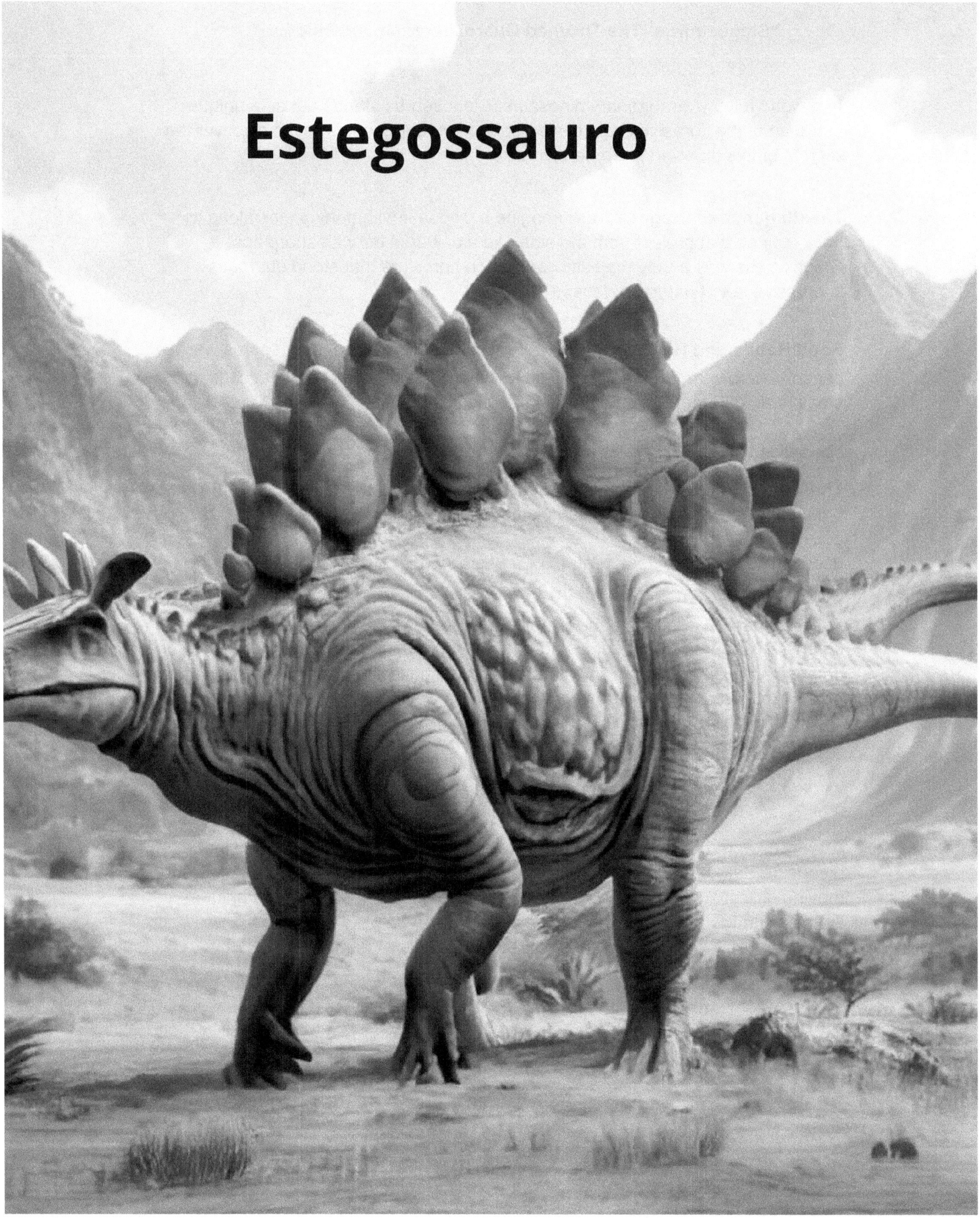

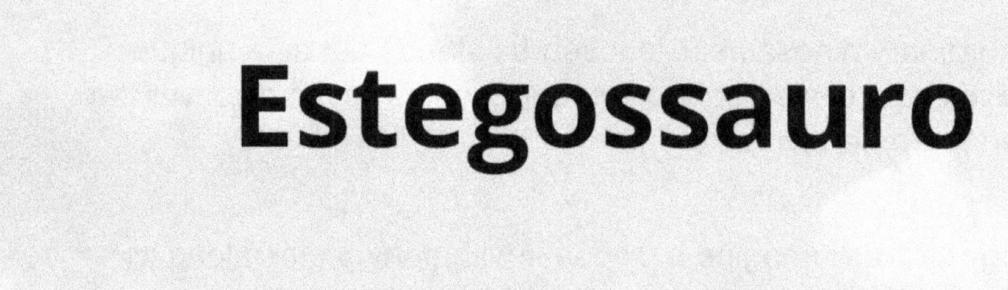

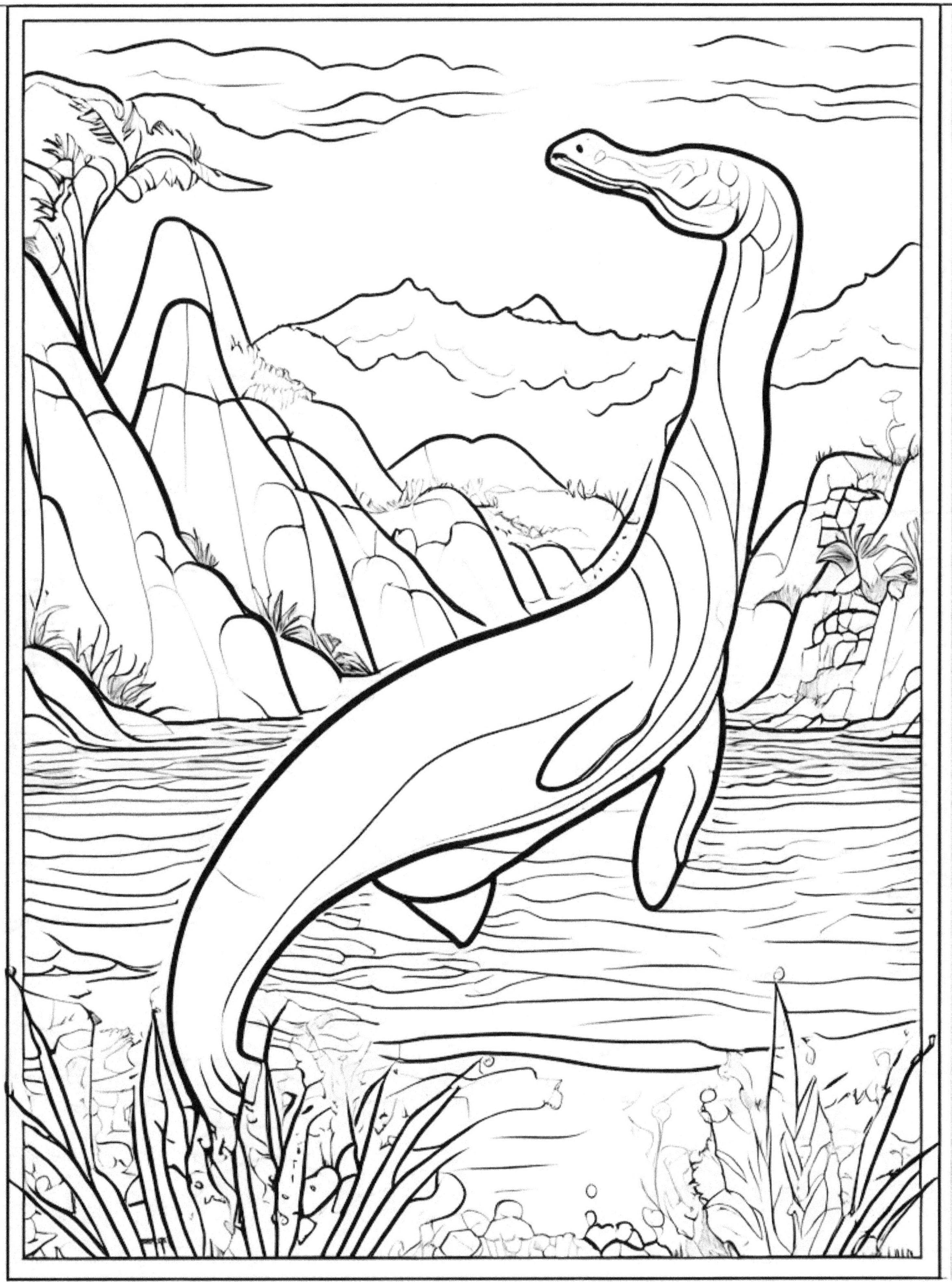

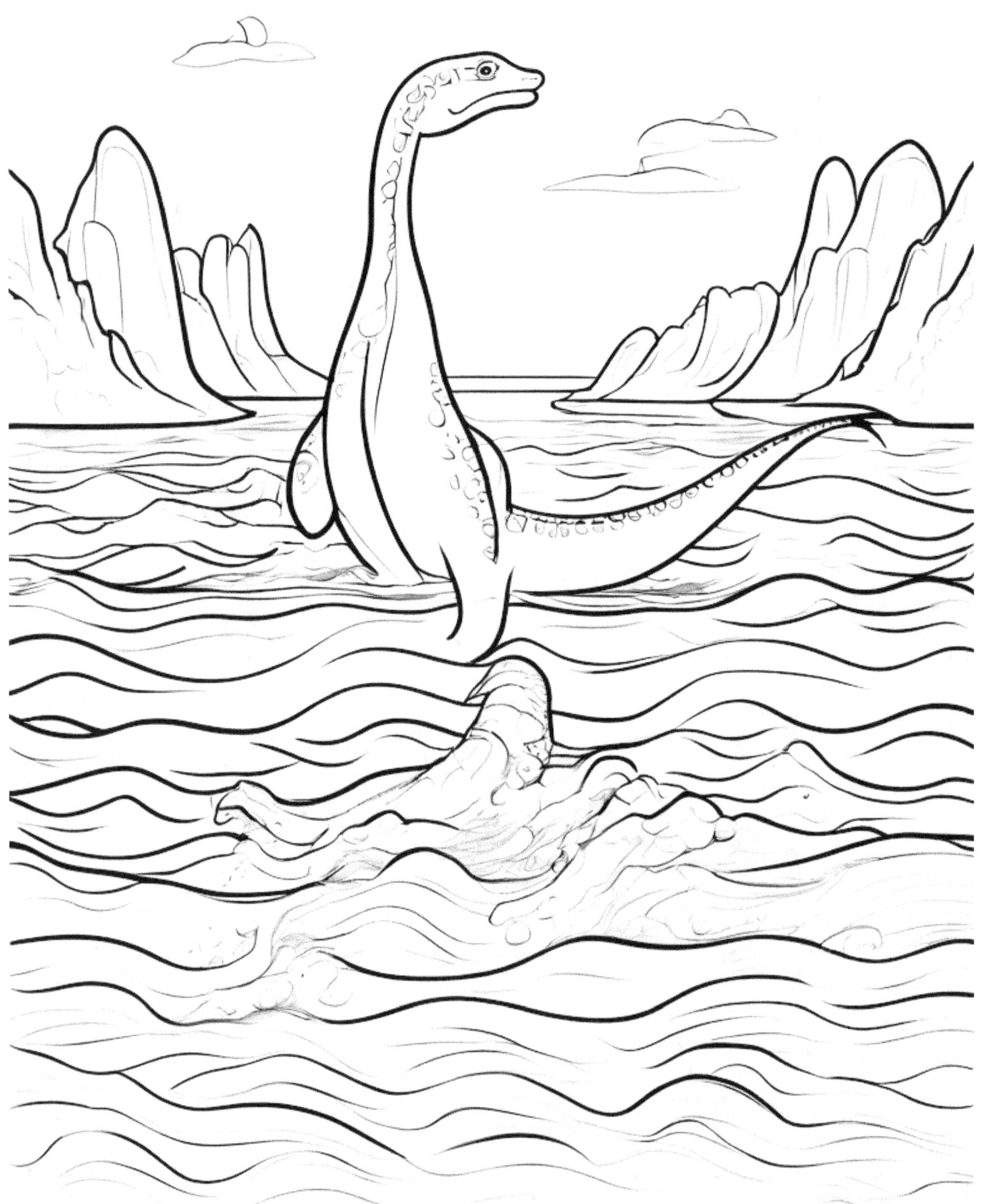

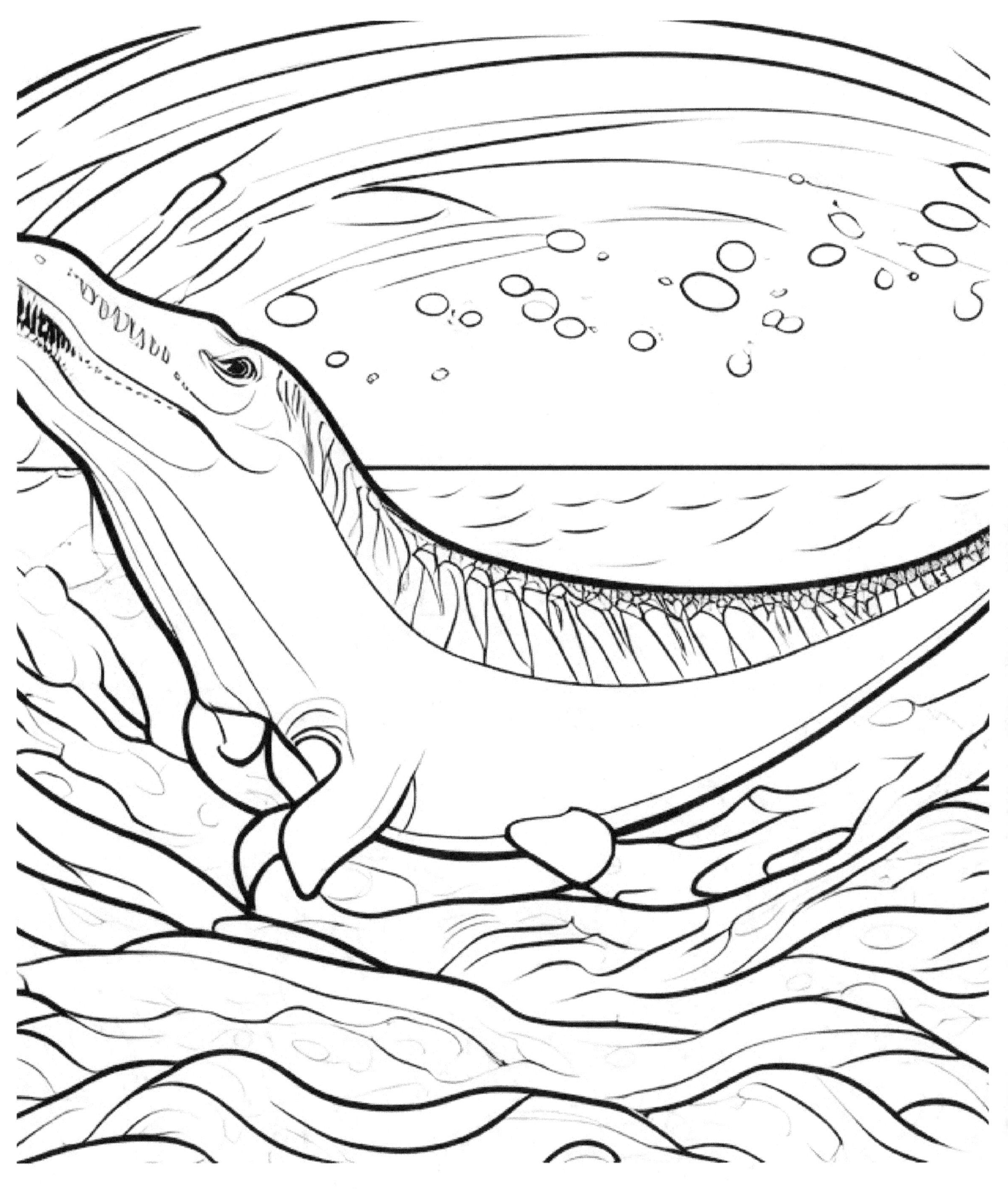

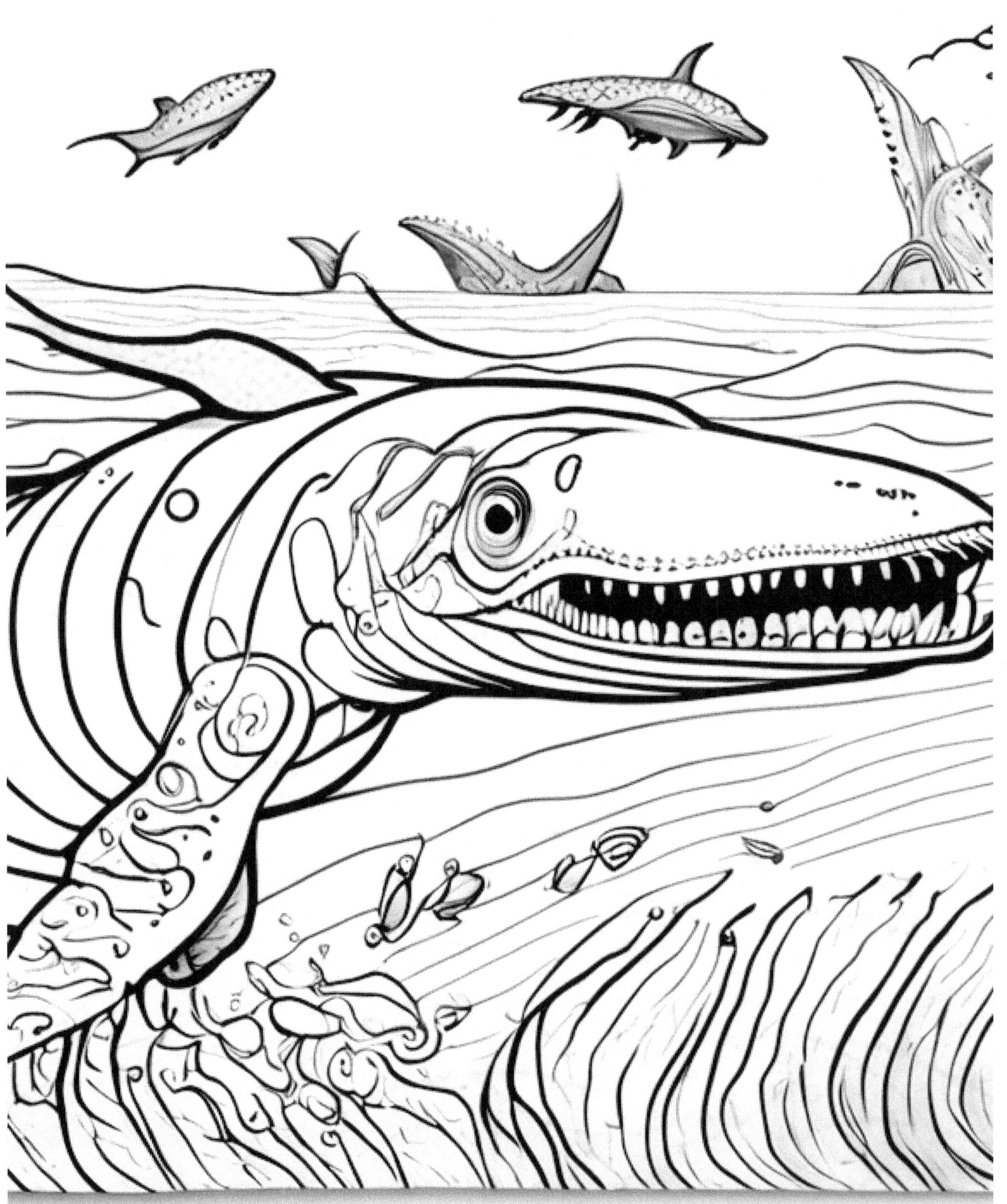

"Pliosaurus: The Monarch of the Jurassic Seas"

In a vast and mysterious ocean, a giant of the seas reigned supreme: the Pliosaurus. Join us on an underwater expedition to discover the secrets of this imposing Jurassic Era marine predator!

The Magnificence of the Pliosaurus: Imagine a colossal marine reptile, with a powerful head and sharp teeth that rivaled those of any land predator. The Pliosaurus was truly the monarch of the Jurassic seas, ruling the waters with its imposing presence.

Food Habits and Efficient Hunting: The Pliosaurus was a fierce predator that fed mainly on fish, but also hunted other large marine animals, including ichthyosaurs and even other pliosaurs. Its powerful jaw and sharp teeth were perfectly adapted for efficient hunting.

How They Lived in the Oceans: Pliosaurs were creatures adapted to oceanic life, with hydrodynamic bodies and powerful fins that made them agile swimmers. It is believed that these predators traveled great distances in search of prey, exploring the vast Jurassic oceans.

Places Where They Reigned: Pliosaur fossils have been found in various parts of the world, indicating that these marine giants were inhabitants of global oceans. Their fossil footprints marked the records of Jurassic Era marine life.

The Age of Dominated Oceans: As we explore the age of Pliosaurs, we are transported to a world where the oceans were dominated by impressive creatures. Imagine the blue depths teeming with life, with the Pliosaurus as one of the top predators, ruling the seas with majesty.

Underwater Adventure: Adventurous kids, dive with us on this underwater adventure! Visualize the depths of the Jurassic oceans, where the Pliosaurus cuts through the waters with grace and power. Join us to explore the mysteries and wonders of the Pliosaurus, the monarch of the Jurassic seas!

Pliossauro

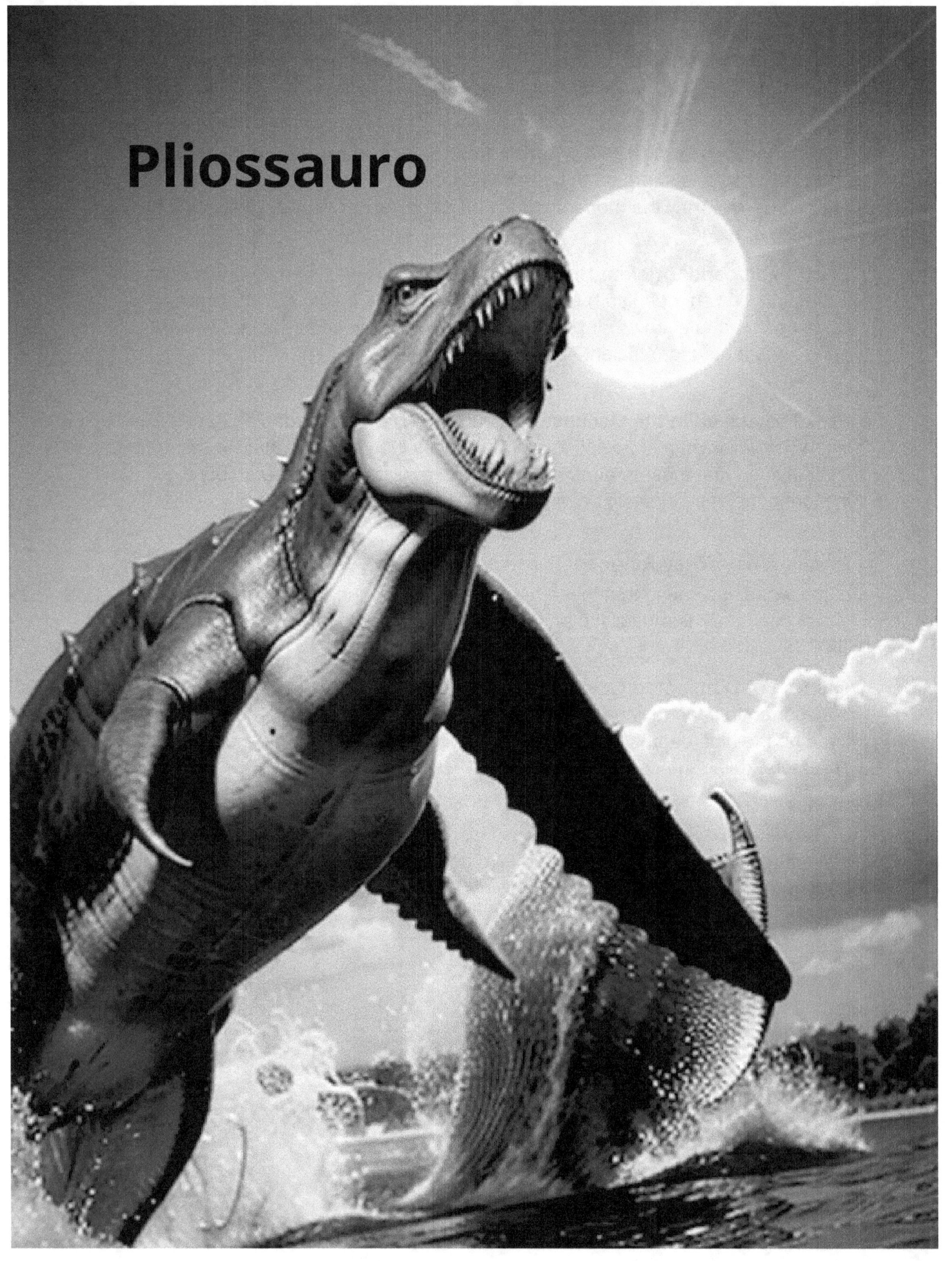

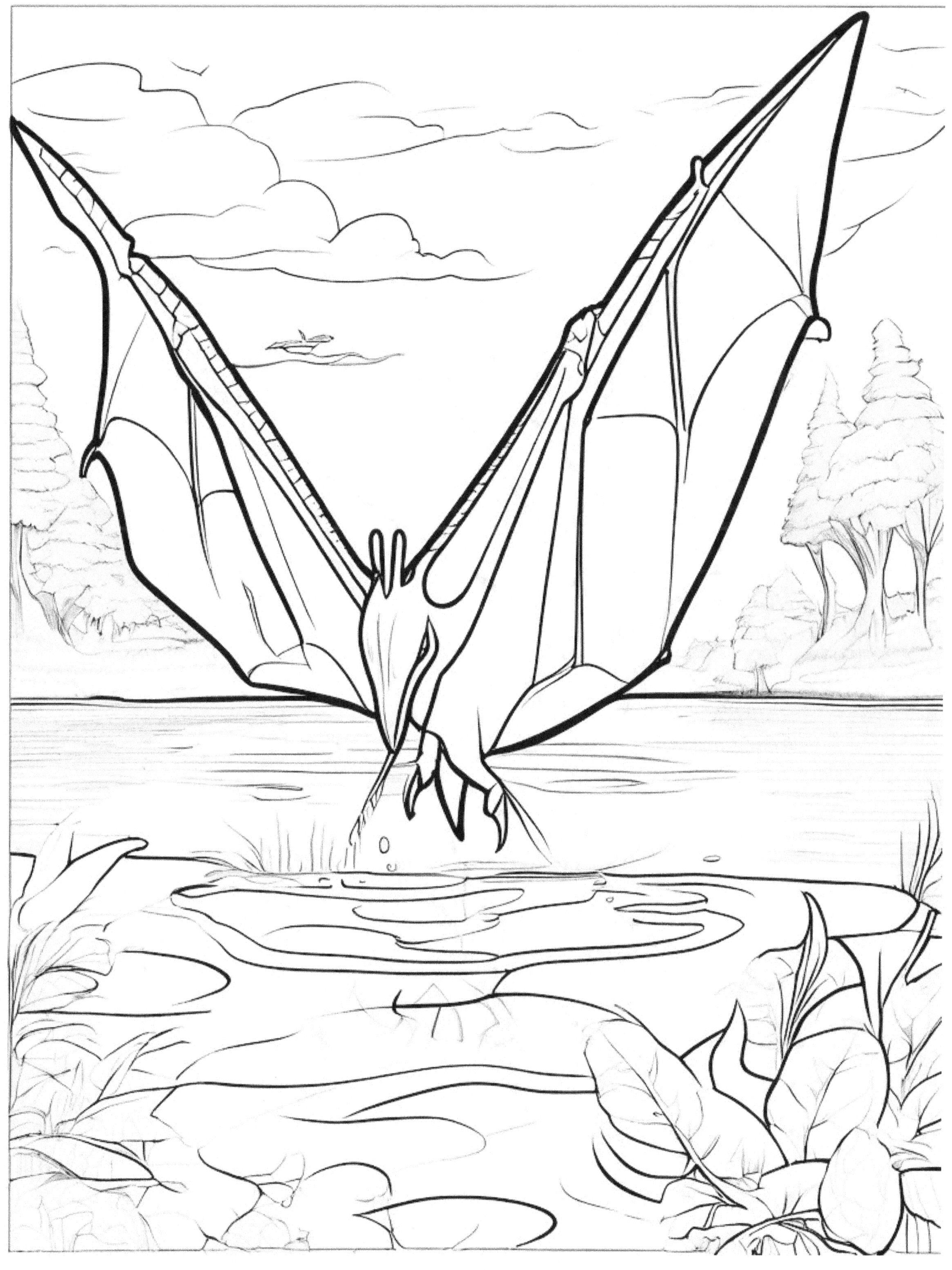

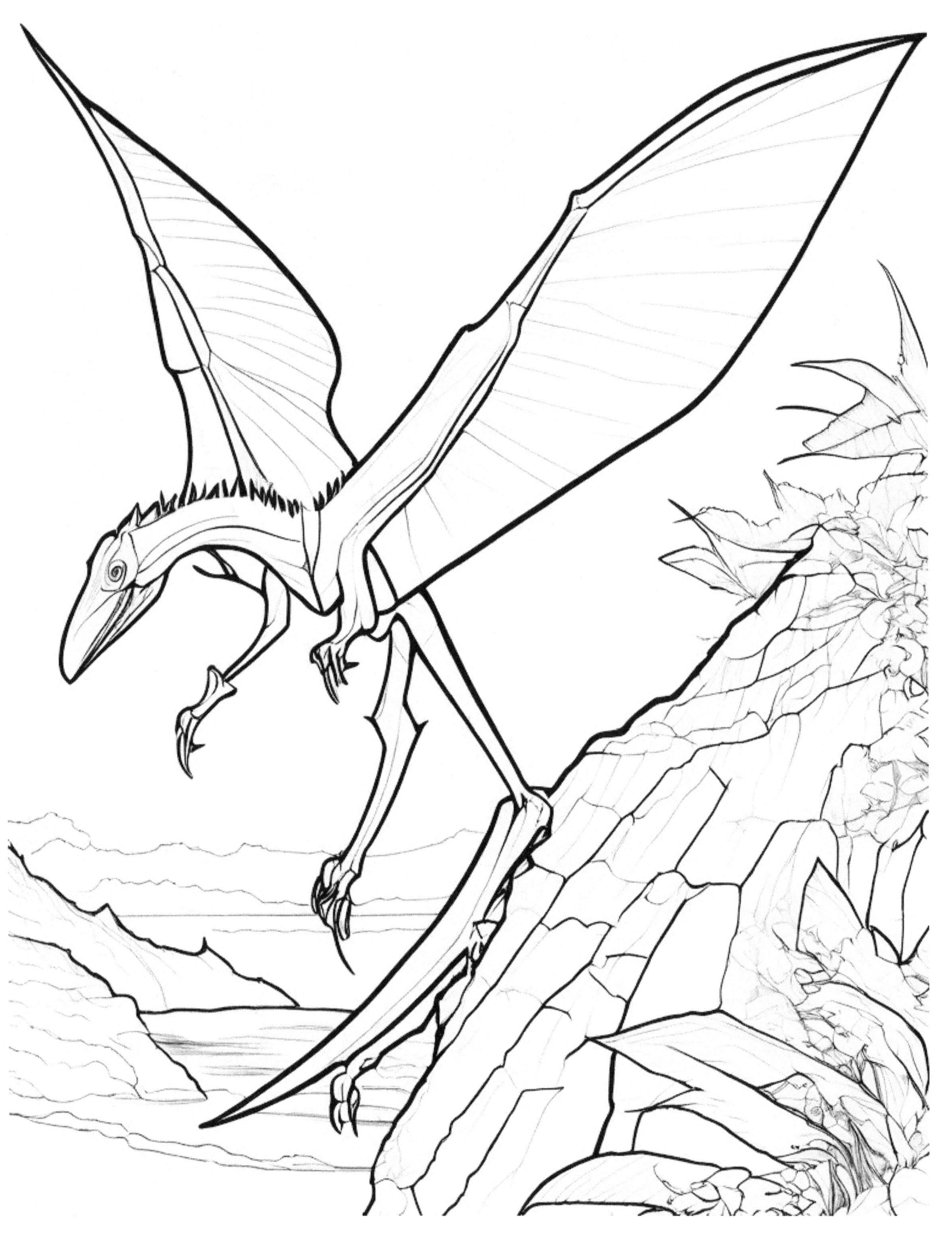

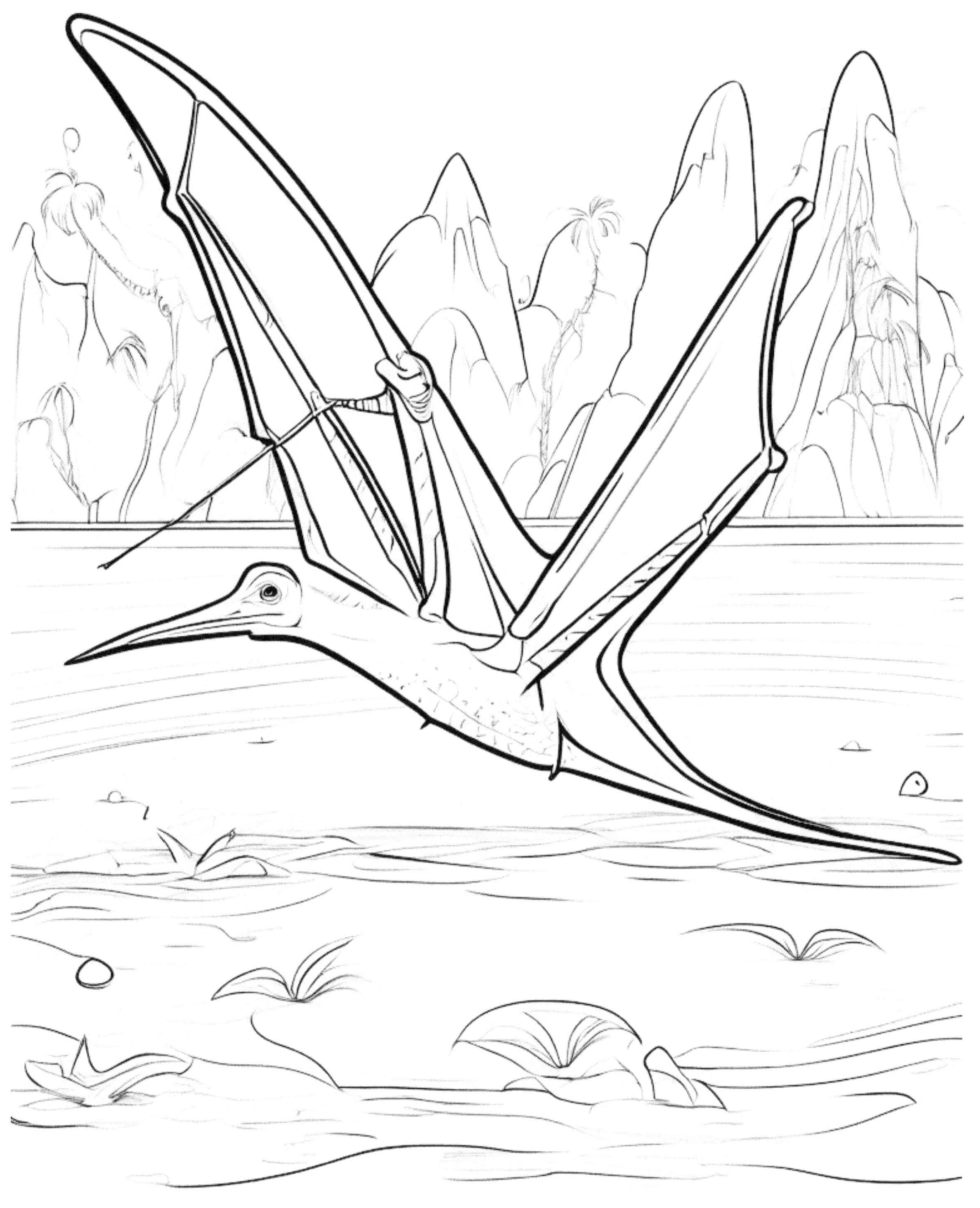

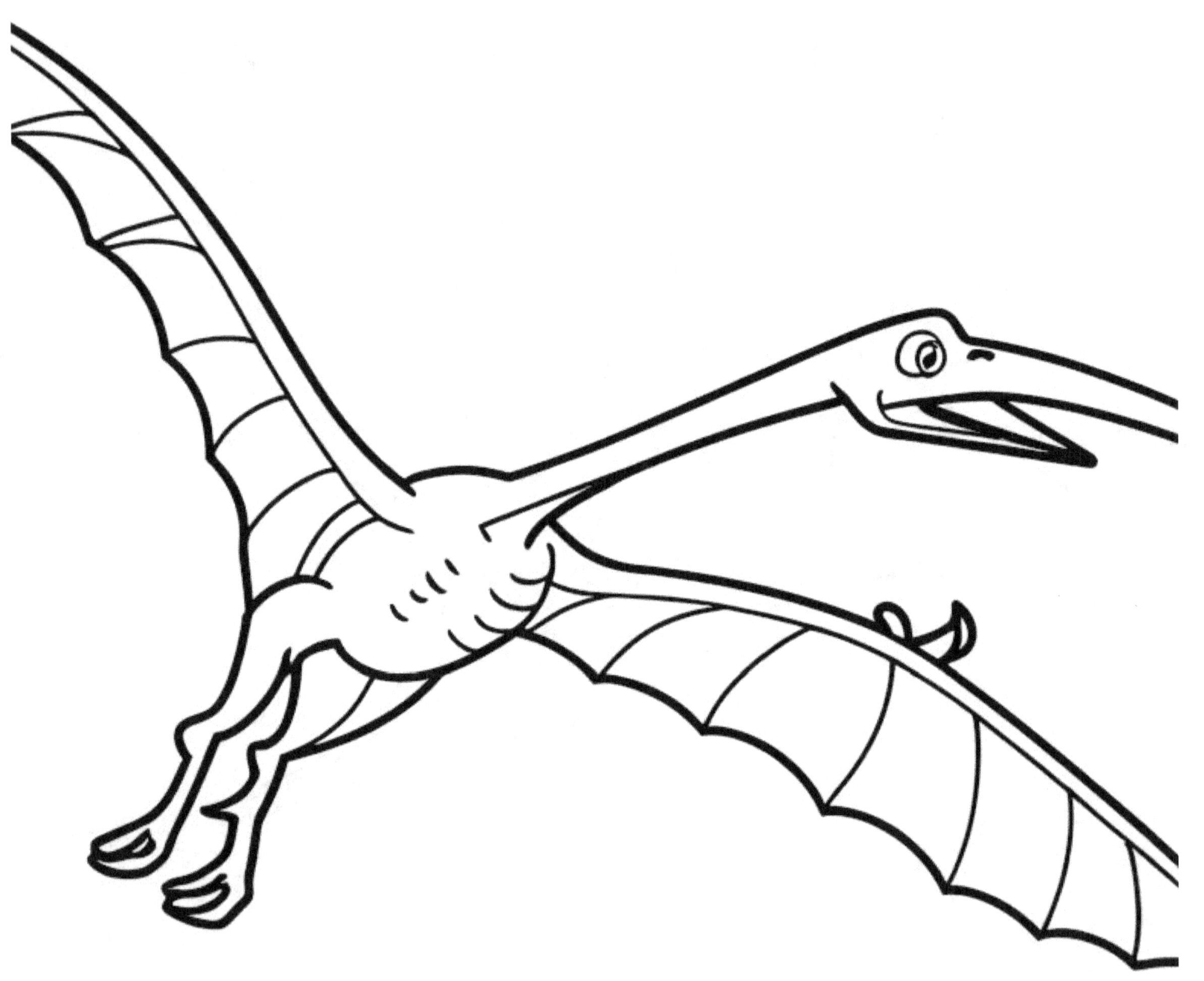

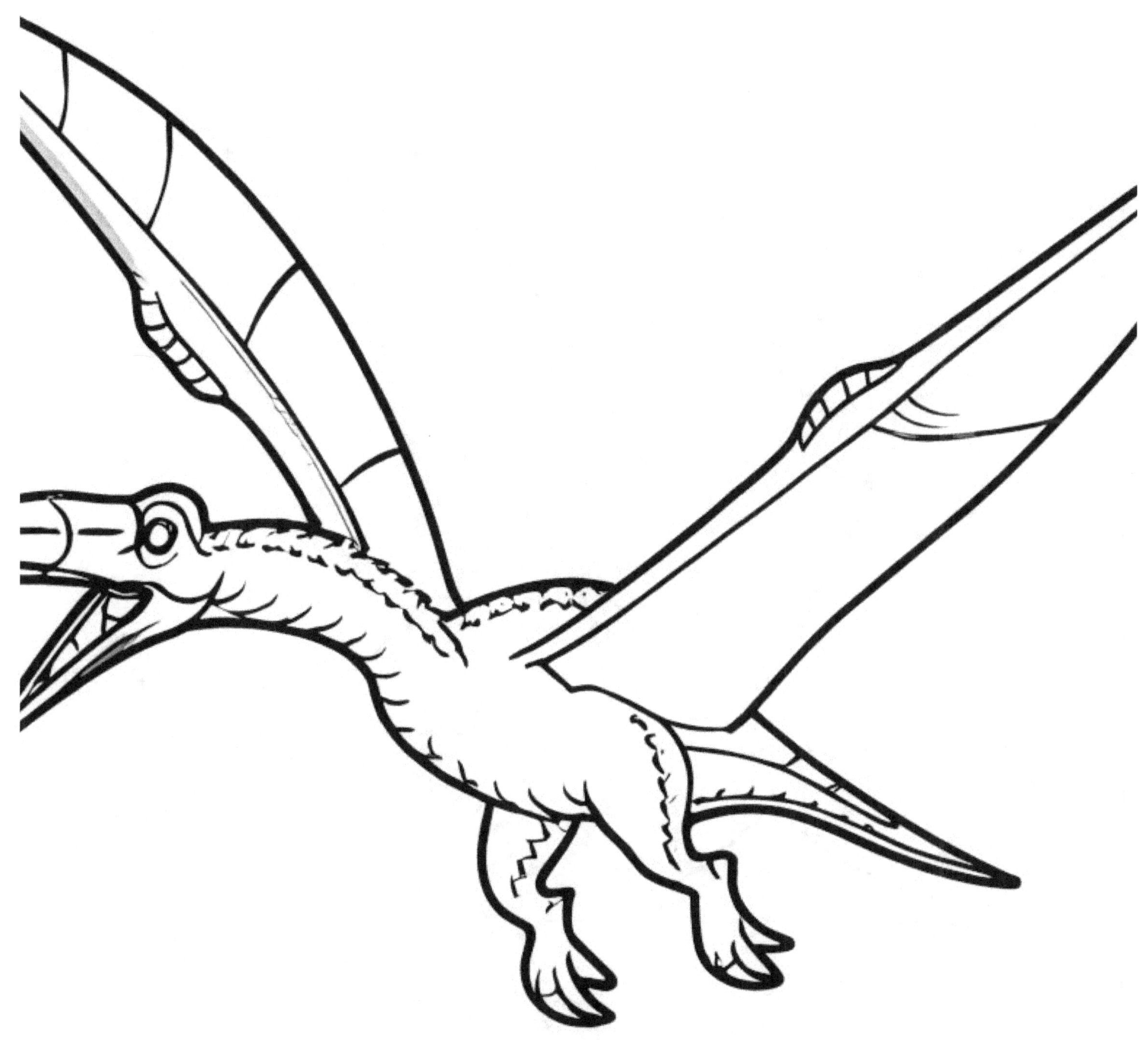

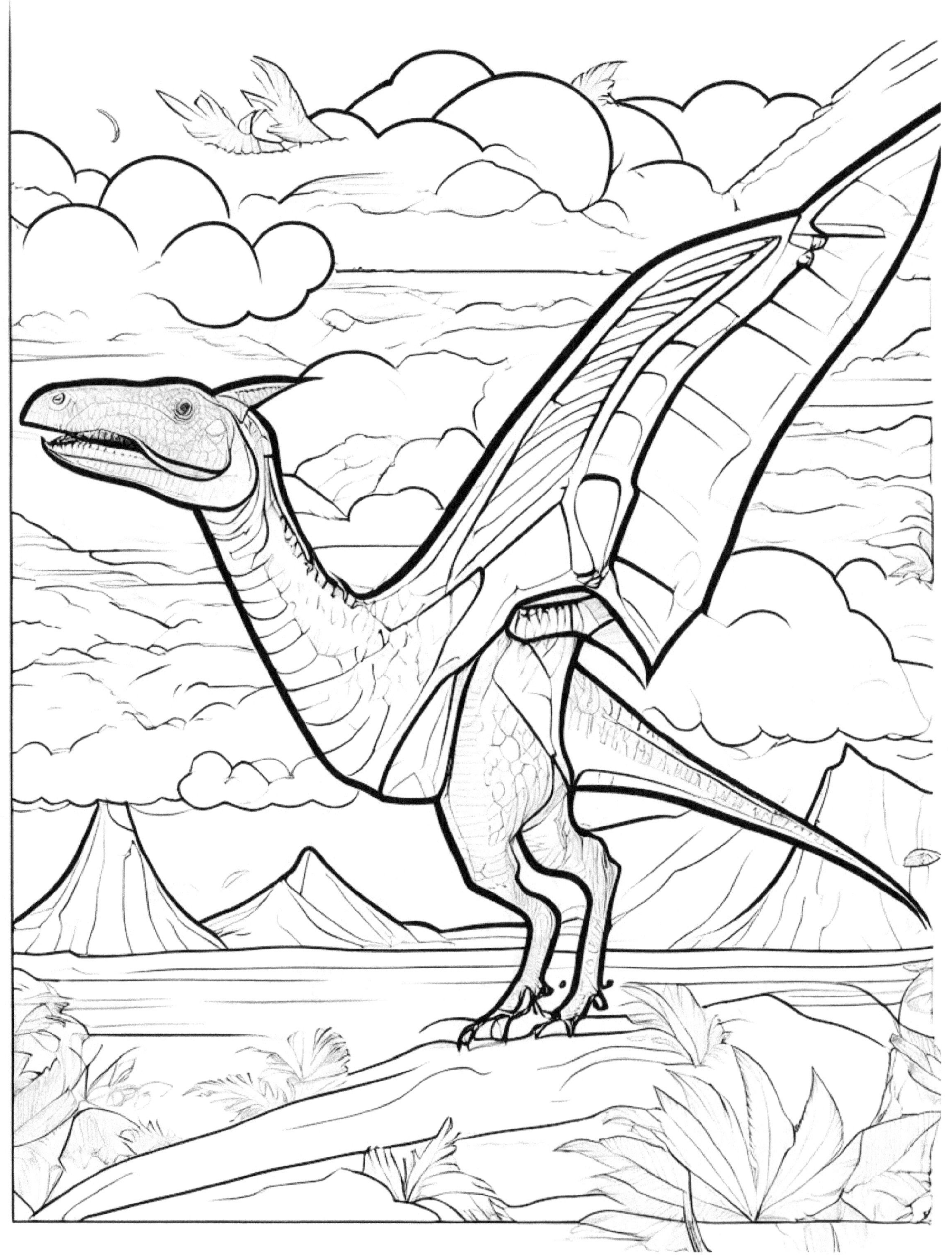

"Pterodactyl: Lord of the Skies in the Age of Dinosaurs"

At a time when the skies were reigned by winged creatures, the Pterodactyl stood out as a true master of the air. Come with us on this exciting adventure to discover the secrets of this incredible flying reptile from the Age of Dinosaurs!

The Imposing Wings of the Pterodactyl: Imagine a reptile with wings so wide and imposing that they could reach wingspans of up to 7 meters. The Pterodactyl, despite not technically being a dinosaur, was an incredible flying reptile that defied expectations with its elegant wings.

Food Habits in the Sky: While many dinosaurs were land creatures, the Pterodactyl was a master of the sky. Its diet consisted mainly of fish and other marine animals that it captured with its sharp beak while flying over the seas and rivers.

How It Lived in the Skies: The Pterodactyl was a skilled glider and flew using its membranous wings, similar to those of a bat. With paws adapted to grasp prey and move around on dry land, it could explore both the heavens and the earth, adding a unique dimension to its life.

Places where it flew: Pterodactyl fossils have been found in various parts of the world, suggesting that these flying reptiles inhabited coastal and river environments. Rivers and oceans were their domain, and their wings allowed them to explore vast expanses in search of food.

Dancing in the Skies: Children, close your eyes and imagine the Pterodactyl dancing in the skies. Visualize your wings stretching majestically as you glide over glistening waters, expertly catching fish. Their screams echo, creating a unique symphony in the prehistoric landscape.

Adventure in the Blue Skies: Come with us on this adventure through the blue skies of the Age of Dinosaurs! Together we will explore the secrets of the Pterodactyl, the lord of the skies, witnessing his grace and power as he ruled the air. An exciting journey awaits as we uncover the mysteries of this magnificent flying reptile!

Pterodáctilo

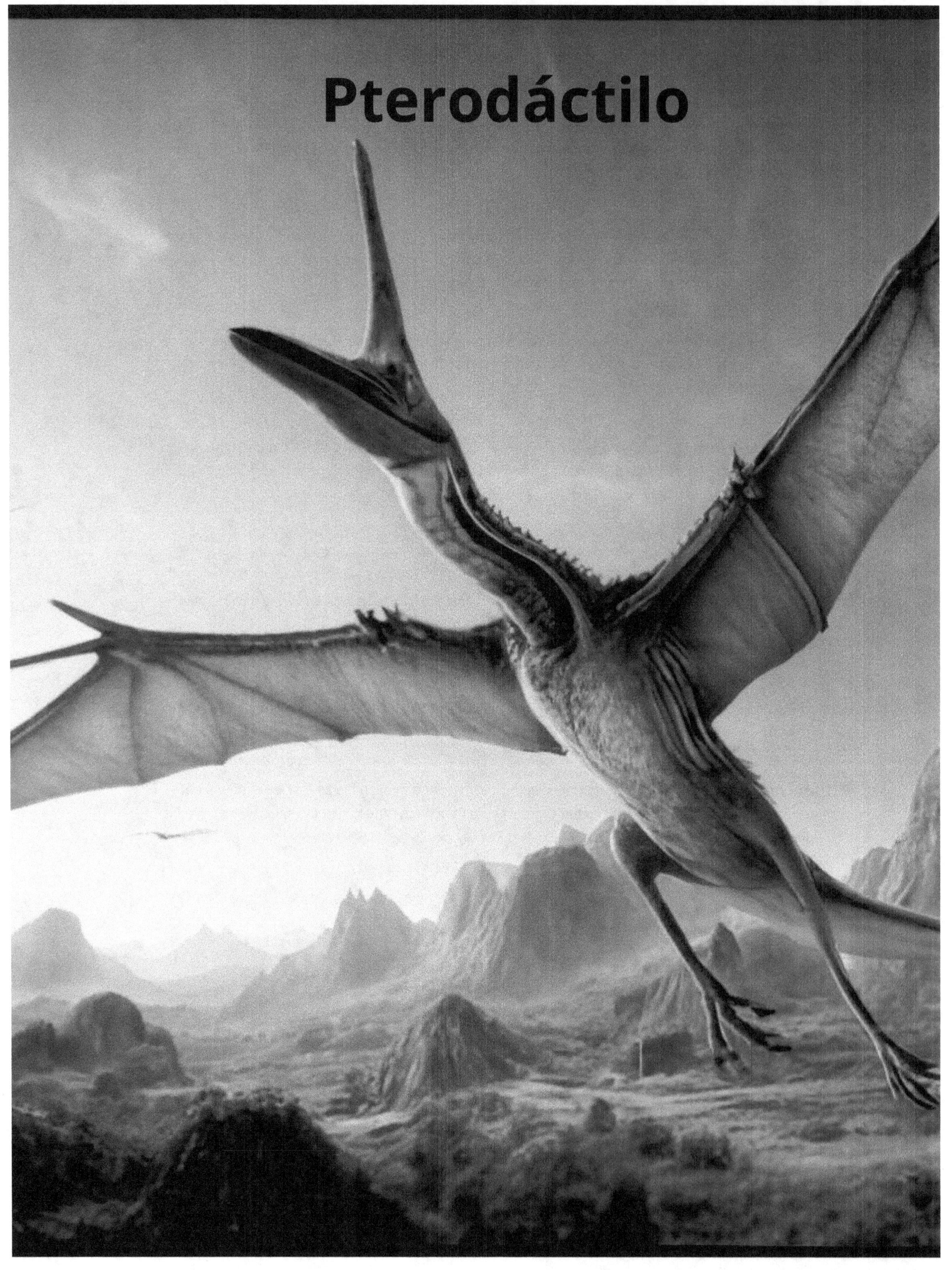

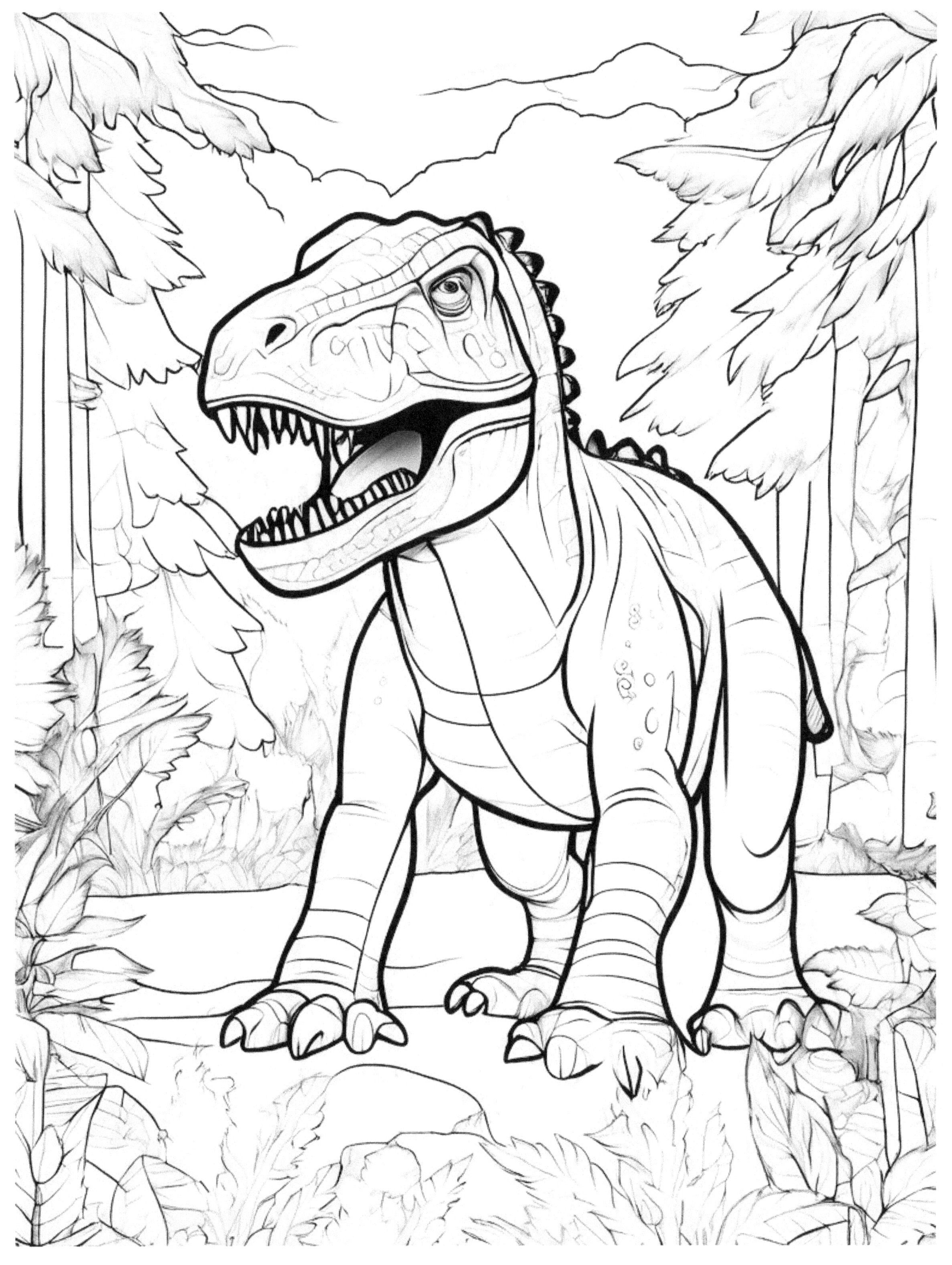

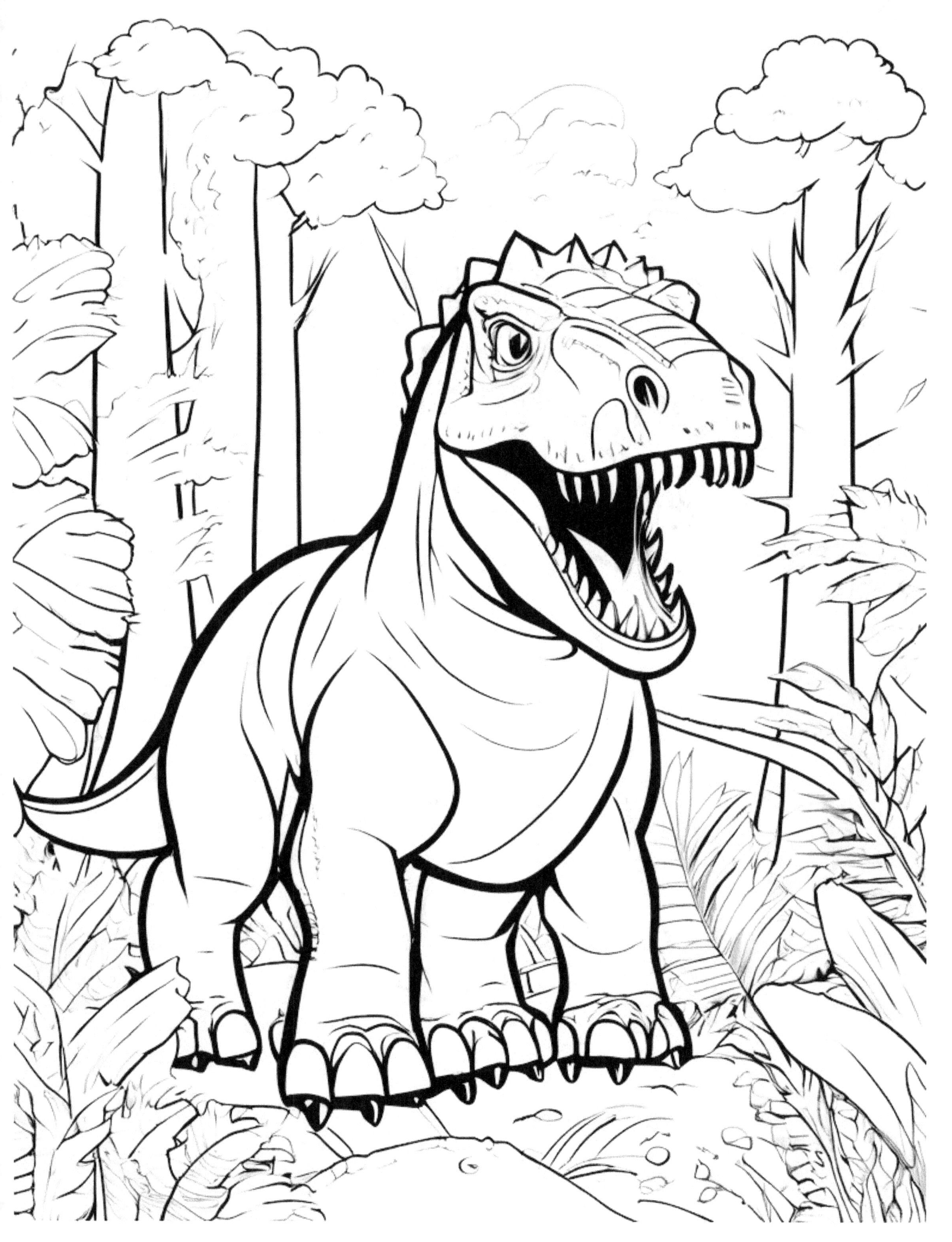

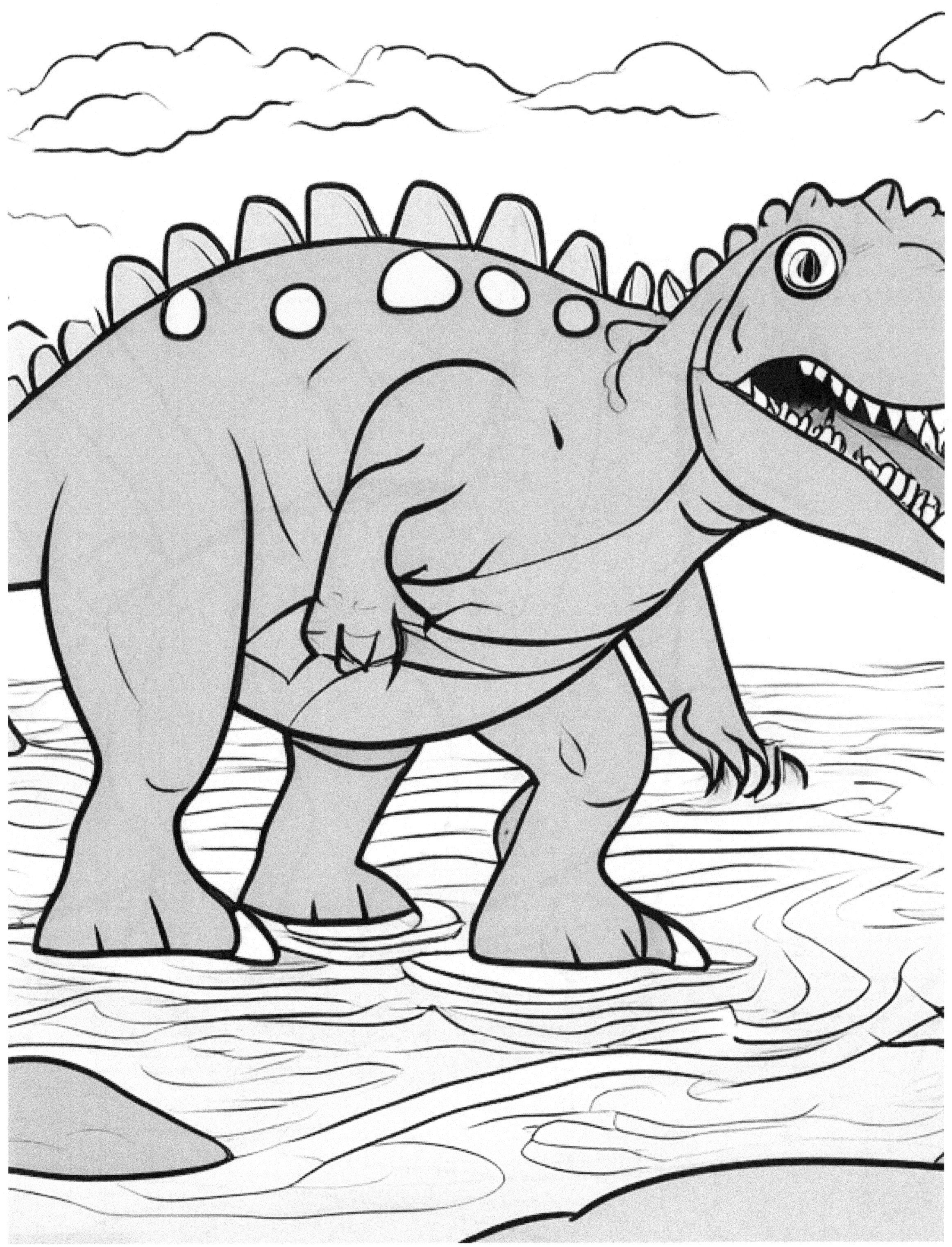

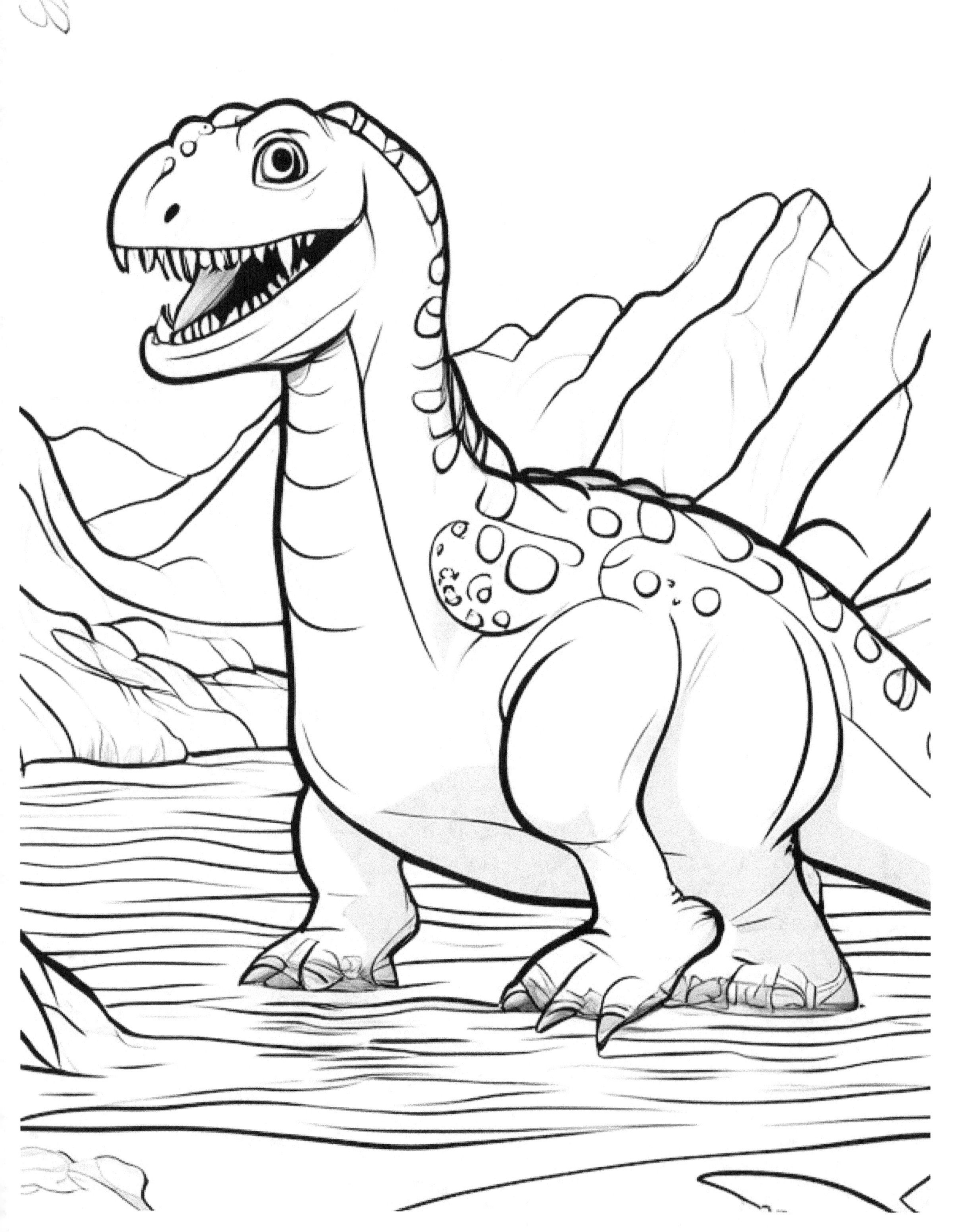

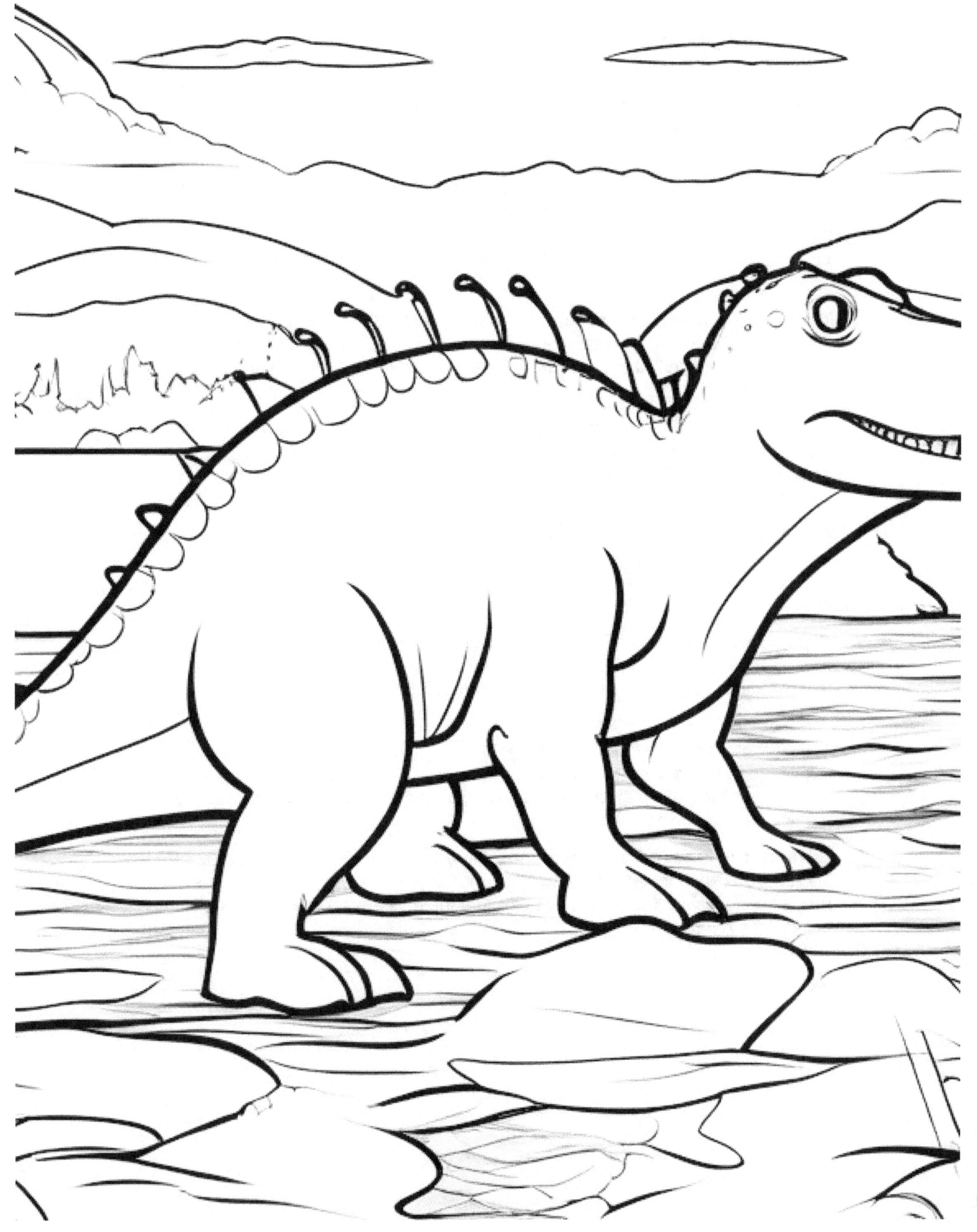

"Purusaurus: The Monarch of the Amazon Rivers"

In the ancient past, when the Amazon was a kingdom of mysteries, a predator reigned supreme in the rivers: the Purussaurus. Join us on a journey through ancient waters to uncover the secrets of this giant of the Amazon rivers!

Purussaurus is known to have been a prehistoric crocodilian of large proportions, but the exact size may vary depending on the specific species. Estimates indicate that some species of Purussaurus could reach lengths of more than 10 meters, being considered formidable predators in aquatic ecosystems at the time.

The Magnificence of Purussaurus: Imagine a colossal aquatic reptile, with an imposing head and an elongated body that glided through the waters with grace. Purussaurus was truly the monarch of the Amazon rivers, displaying unparalleled magnificence.

Food Habits and Efficient Hunting: Purussaurus was a voracious predator, feeding mainly on fish, turtles and other aquatic animals. With sharp teeth and powerful jaws, this giant was an efficient hunter, capable of dominating rivers in search of prey.

Adaptation to Aquatic Life: Unlike its terrestrial relatives, Purussaurus was completely adapted to aquatic life. Its elongated body and short legs indicated a life spent predominantly in water, where it could swim with agility and dexterity.

Places where it reigned: Purussaurus inhabited the rivers and lakes of the ancient Amazon, a region rich in biodiversity and vast aquatic ecosystems. Its fossils tell the story of a time when rivers were ruled by formidable creatures.

The Age of Wild Rivers: As we explore the age of the Purussaurus, we are transported to a world where the Amazon rivers were wild kingdoms, full of life and danger. View this majestic predator gliding through the dark waters, creating a unique spectacle in the aquatic forests.

Adventure in the Amazon Waters: Adventurers, join us on this journey through the Amazon rivers! Imagine the depths of ancient jungles, where Purussaurus reigned majestically. Come with us to explore the mysteries and wonders of this giant of the Amazon rivers!

Purussauro

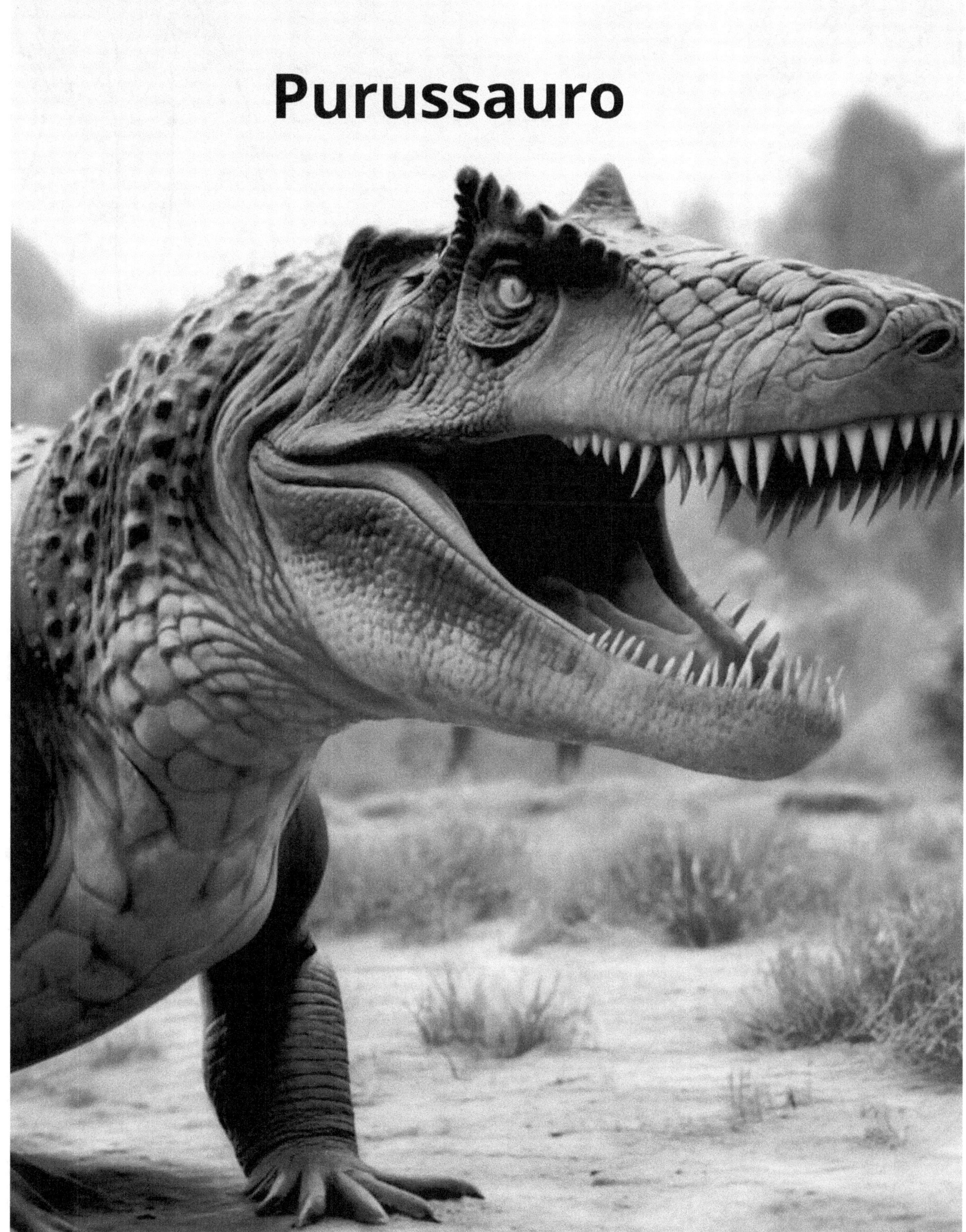

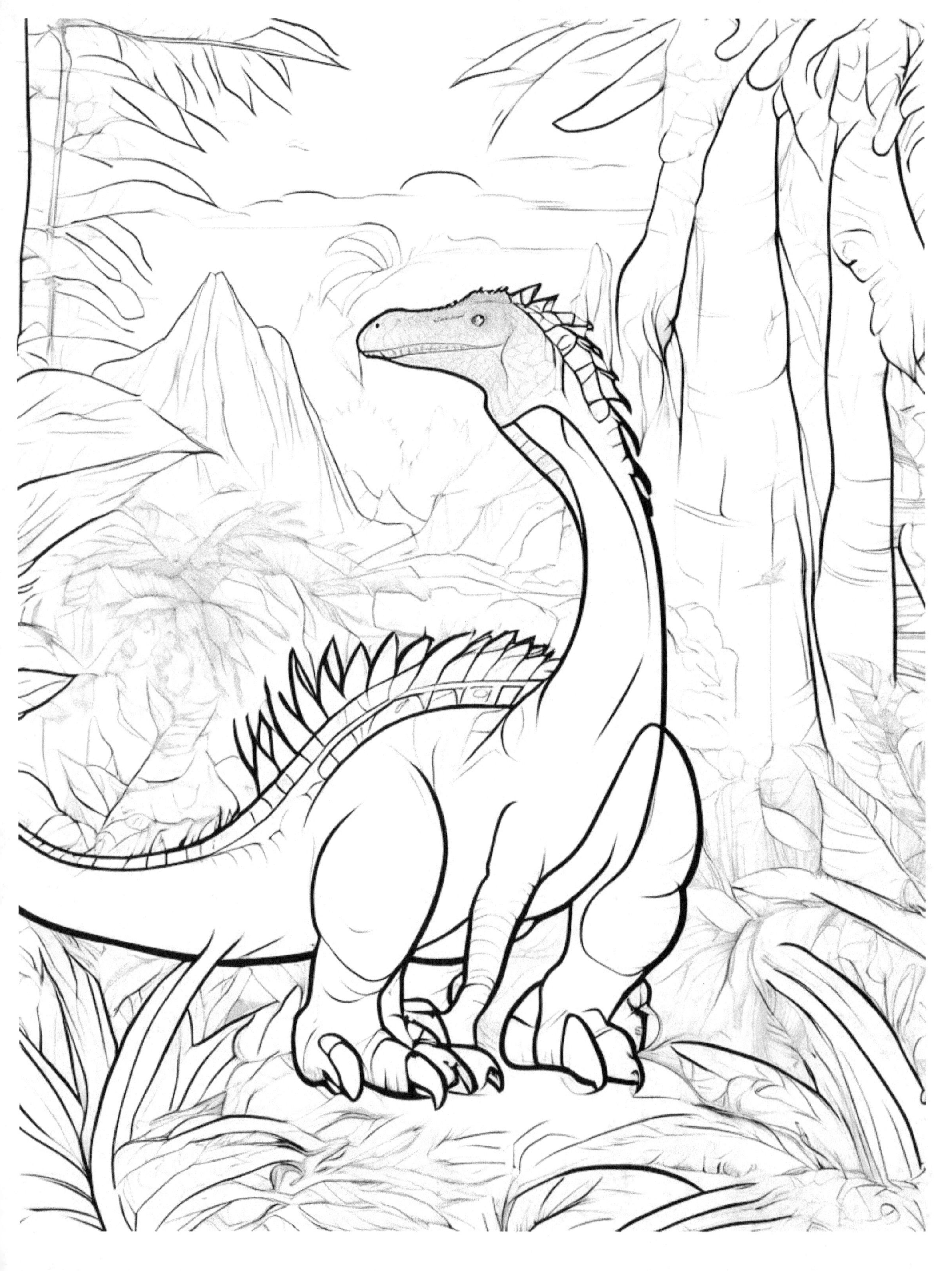

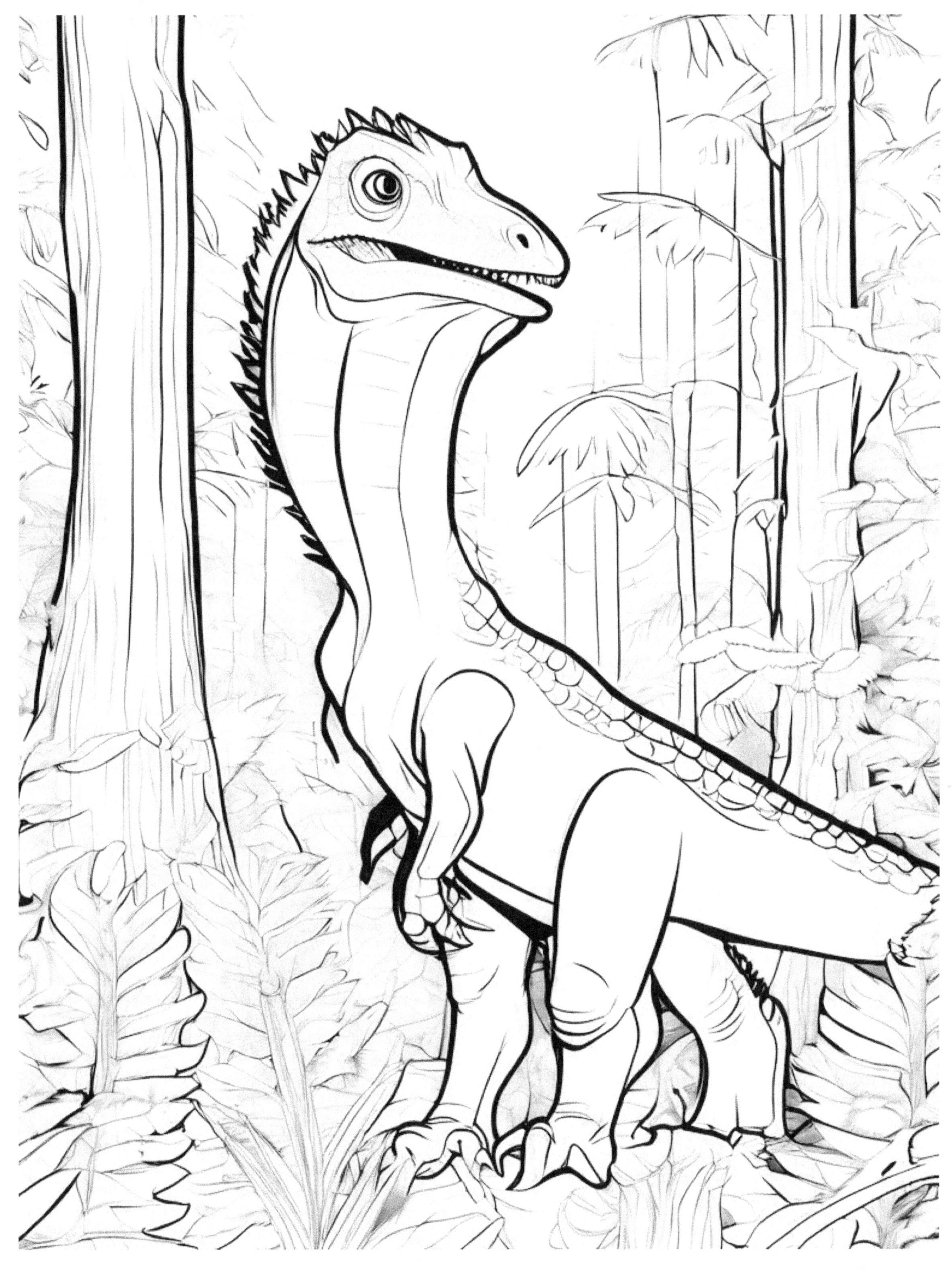

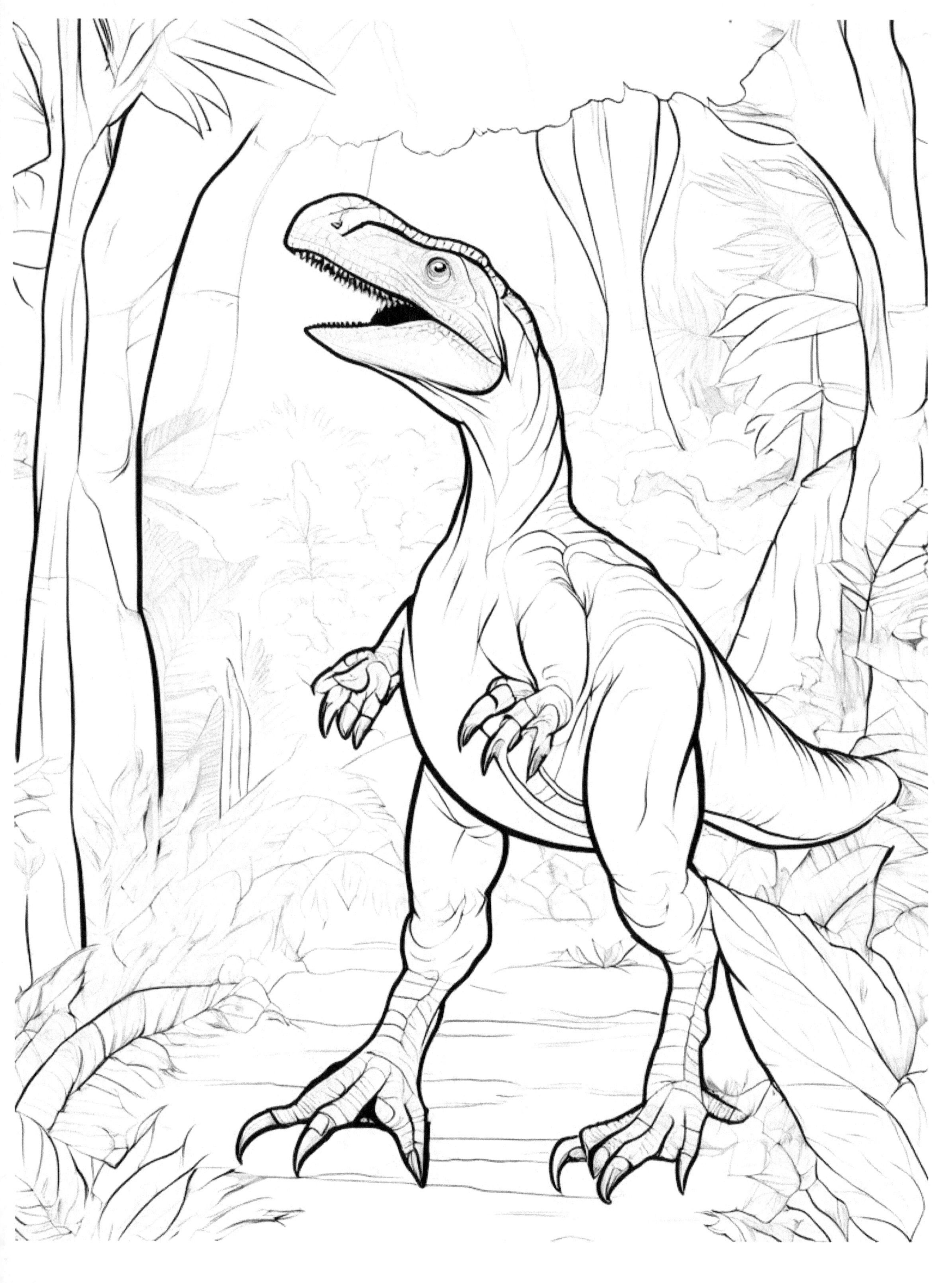

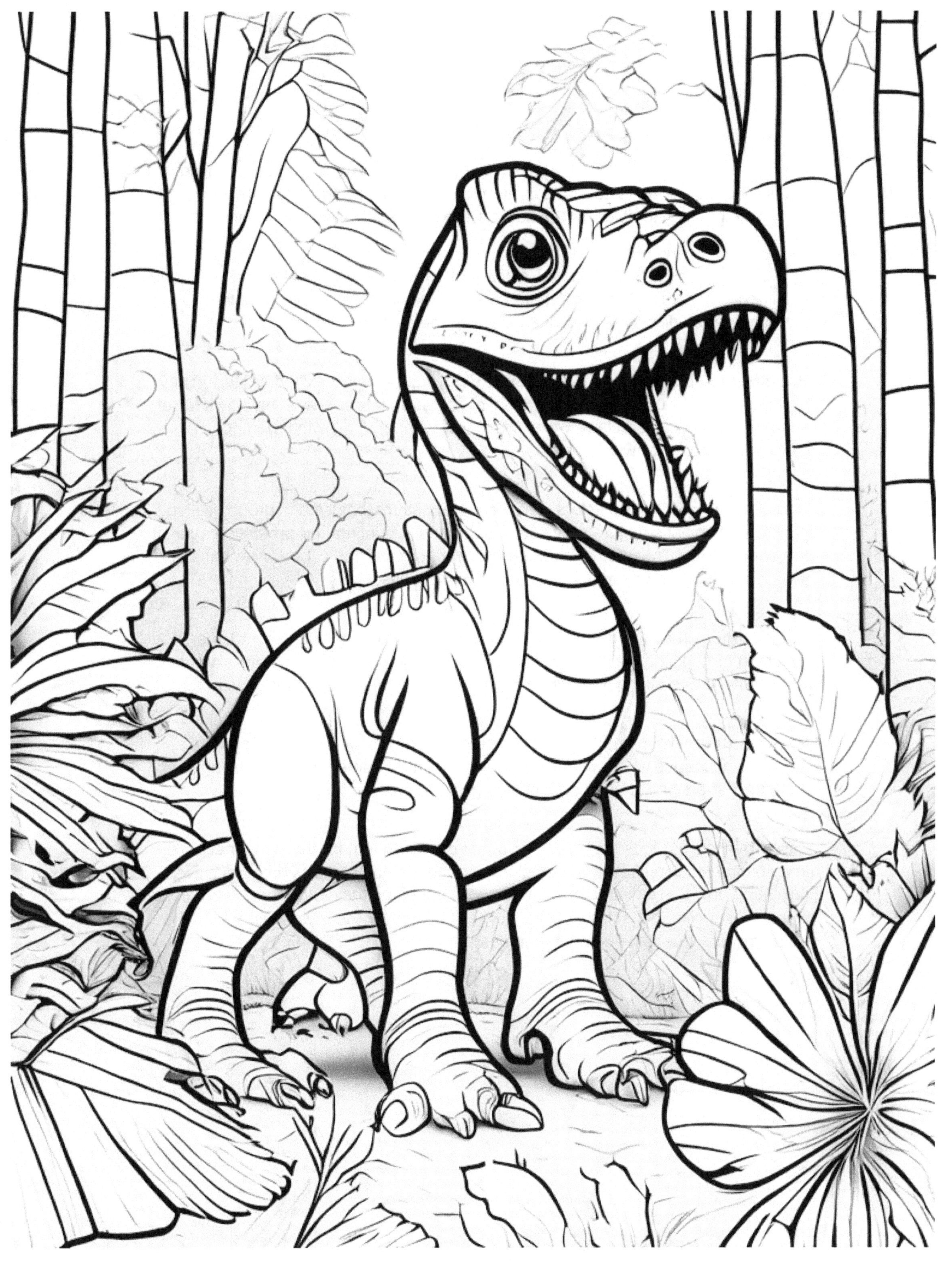

"Velociraptor: Fast Hunters of the Past"

In a distant time, when the world was dominated by dinosaurs, a group of agile and intelligent predators caught our attention: the Velociraptors. Join us on an exciting expedition to discover the secrets of these fast and cunning dinosaurs!

The Elegance of Velociraptors: Velociraptors were small but extremely agile and intelligent dinosaurs. With their sharp claws, muscular legs and elegant feathers, these predators displayed a unique beauty in the dinosaur world.

Food Habits: Despite their modest size, Velociraptors were skilled hunters. They hunted in groups, using coordinated tactics to outrun larger prey. Their jaws full of sharp teeth and curved claws were formidable weapons, allowing them to dismember their prey with precision.

How They Lived: Velociraptors were social dinosaurs that lived in groups called packs. This social structure provided advantages in hunting and protection against larger predators. These dinosaurs are believed to have had cooperative behavior, working together to ensure the success of their forays.

Places where they lived: Velociraptors were inhabitants of different regions, including forests and plains. Fossils indicate that they roamed parts of Asia and North America, adapting to different environments during the Cretaceous period.

Pack Hunting: When imagining Velociraptors in action, we are transported to ancient landscapes where these intelligent dinosaurs hunted in packs, using advanced strategies to overcome challenges and ensure the group's survival.

Fast Adventures: Kids, get ready for a fast-paced adventure through time! Let's imagine the thrilling chases of Velociraptors, the sounds of their communicative calls, and how these dinosaurs formed social bonds as they explored the prehistoric world. Come with us on this exciting journey to discover the mysteries of Velociraptors, true fast hunters of the past!

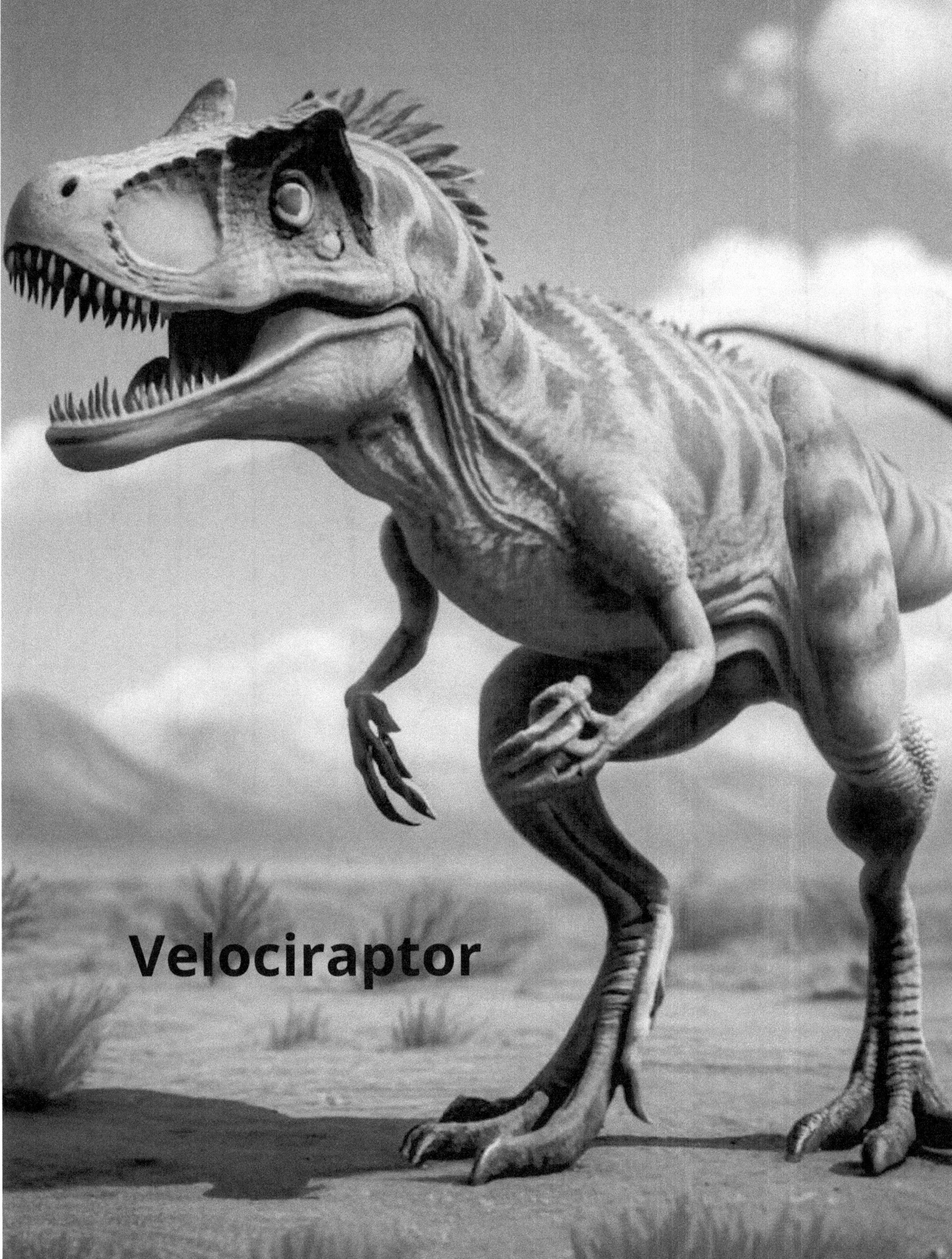
Velociraptor

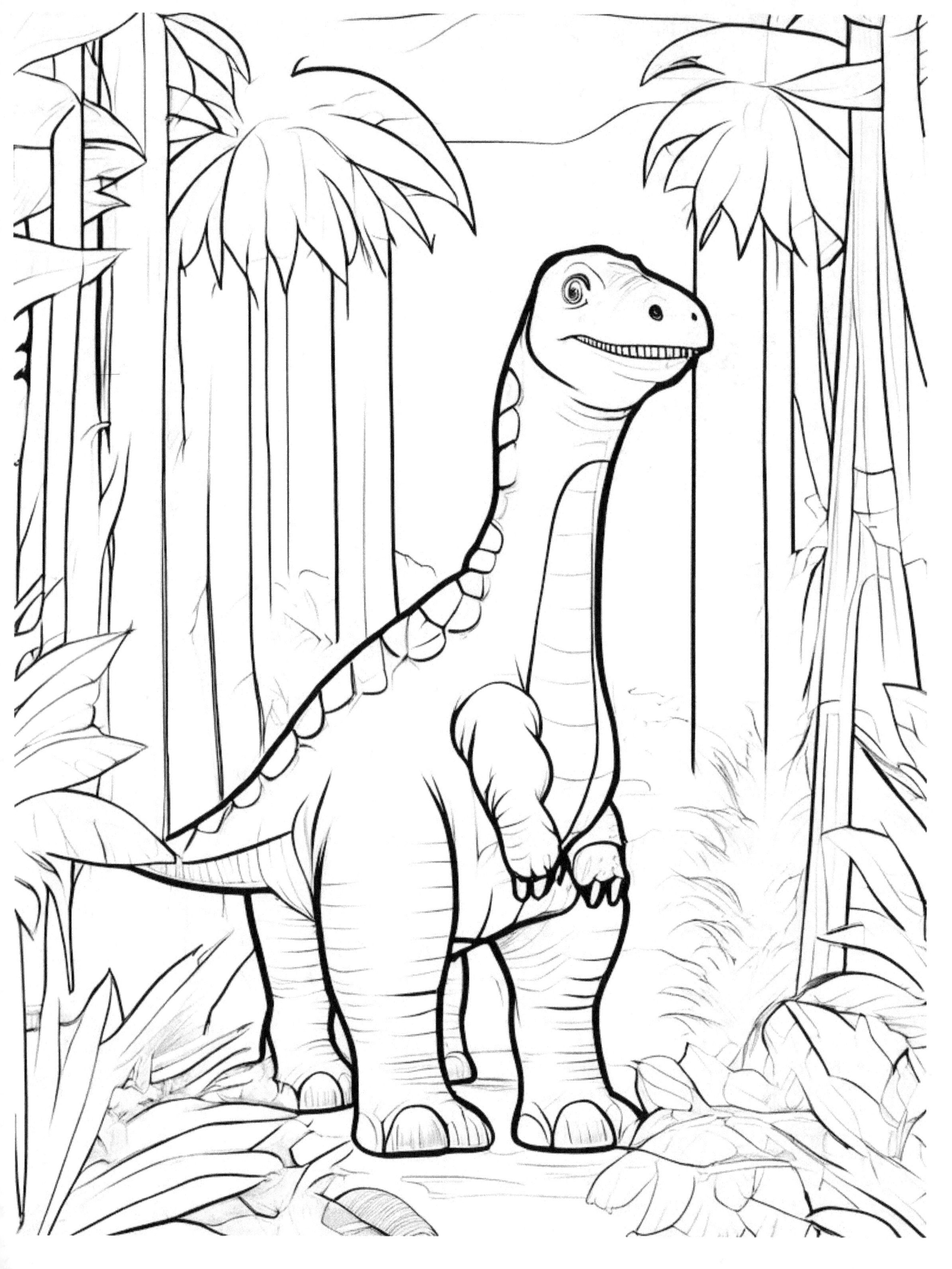

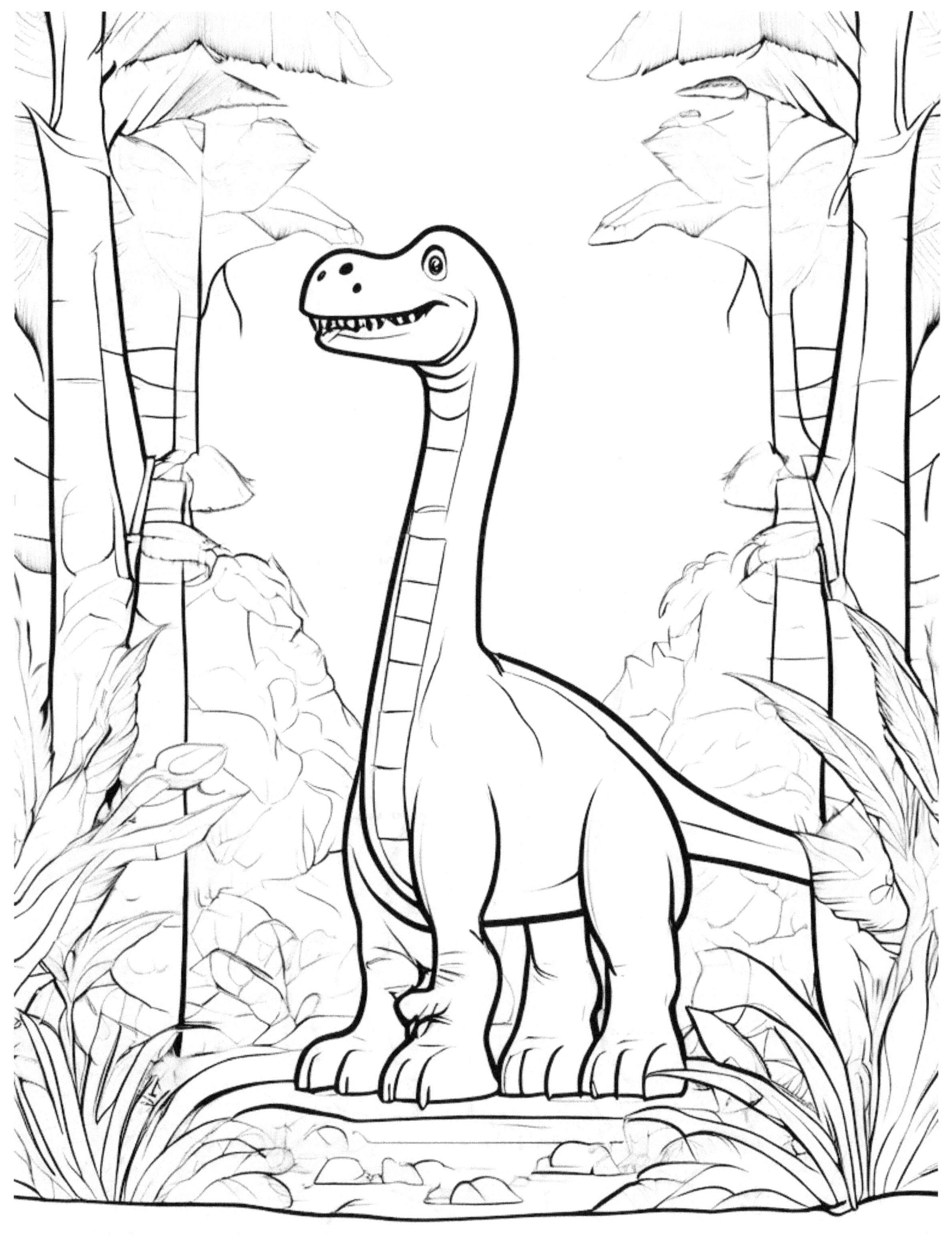

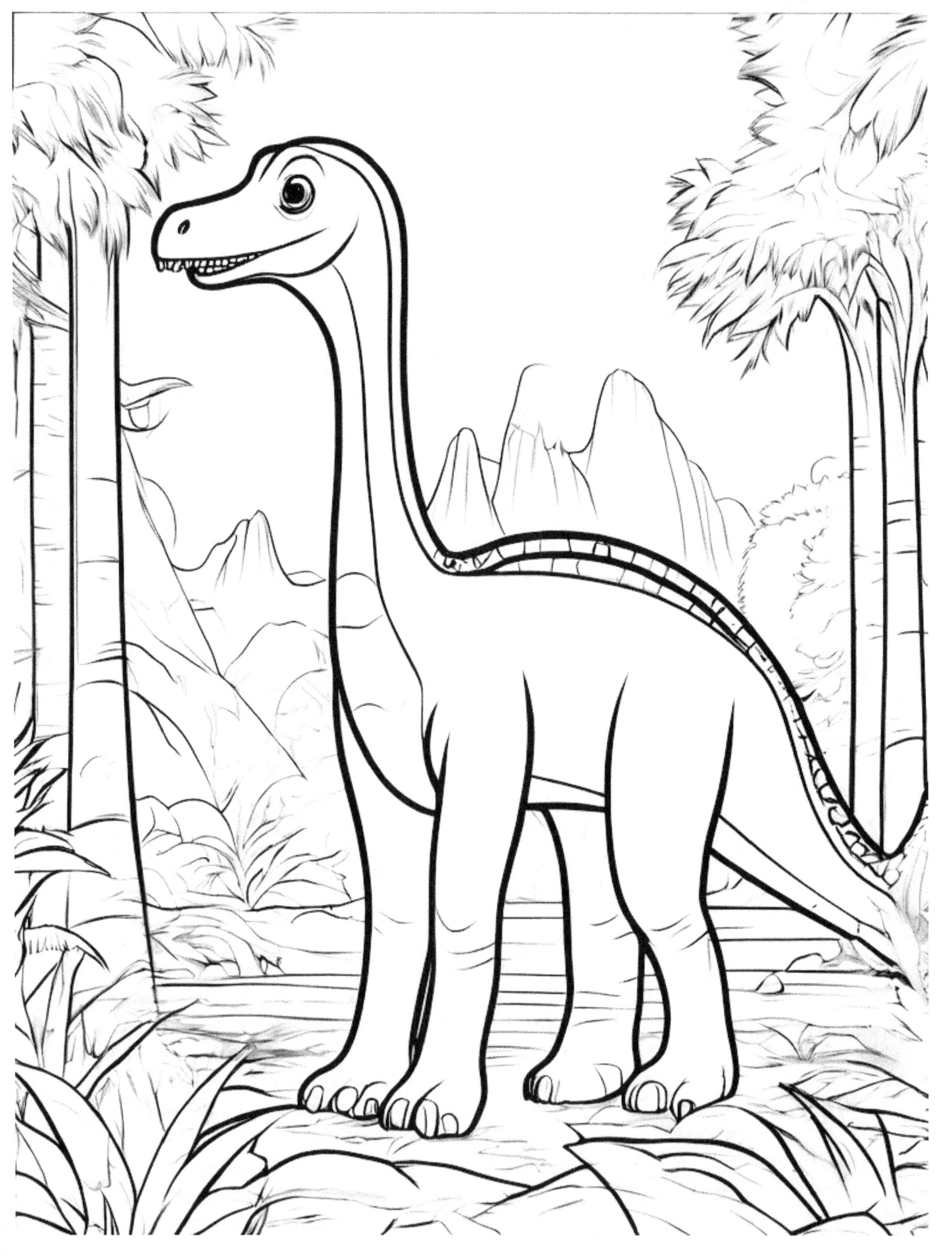

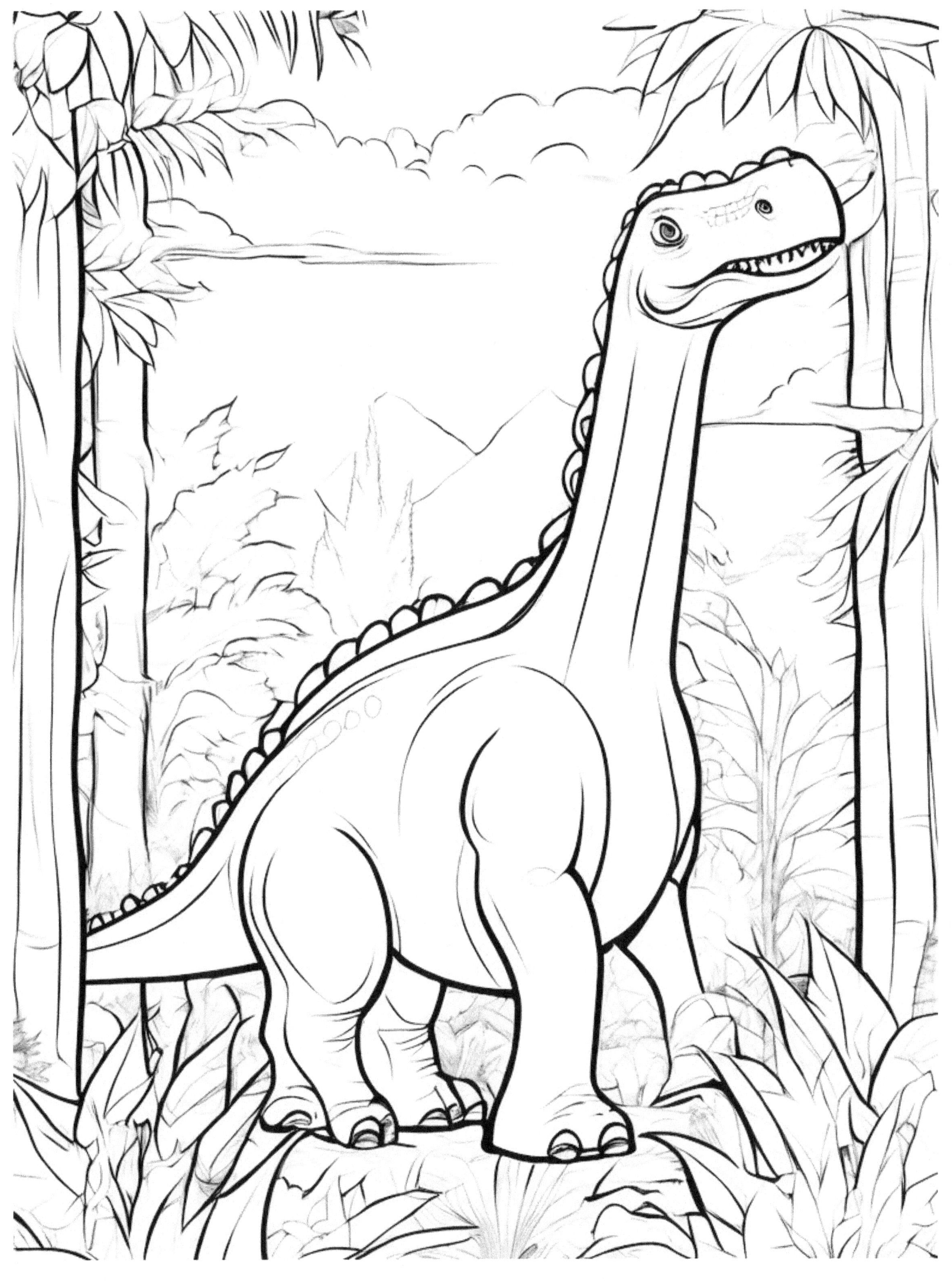

Brachiosaurus: The Friendly Giant of Heights"

In a time where dinosaurs reigned and landscapes were dominated by imposing creatures, a gentle and majestic giant stood out for its impressive heights: the Brachiosaurus. Join us on this expedition through the serene life of this giant herbivore!

The Greatness of Brachiosaurus: Brachiosaurus was truly a colossus among dinosaurs. With an extraordinarily long neck and robust legs, this herbivore reached astonishing heights, becoming one of the most iconic figures of the dinosaur era.

Food Habits: Despite its imposing size, Brachiosaurus was a peaceful herbivore that fed mainly on plants. Its long neck allowed it to reach leaves in the tops of tall trees, making it an expert at feeding on the highest parts of plants.

How They Lived: Brachiosaurs lived in social groups, where they shared information about food sources and protection from predators. These giant dinosaurs had a calm nature, and life in a herd contributed to safety, especially for the youngest.

Places Where They Lived: Brachiosaurus fossils have been found in various parts of the world, suggesting that these giants inhabited different regions during the Jurassic period. Forests and plains were the main environments of these long-necked dinosaurs.

A World in the Heights: Imagine yourself walking through ancient landscapes, where the horizon was adorned by the immense necks of Brachiosaurus towering above the trees. These peaceful giants lived high above, creating a truly remarkable spectacle.

The exact size of Brachiosaurus is a subject of debate among paleontologists, and the estimate can vary. However, on average, it is believed that Brachiosaurus could reach heights of around 15 to 18 meters. If we consider the total length, including the neck and tail, some specimens may have exceeded 25 meters in length.

Treetop Adventures: Kids, get ready for an exciting treetop adventure with Brachiosaurus! Visualize the serenity of these giant dinosaurs as they feed and share life in the heights. Come with us on this journey to explore the mysteries and grandeur of Brachiosaurus, the friendly giant of the heights!

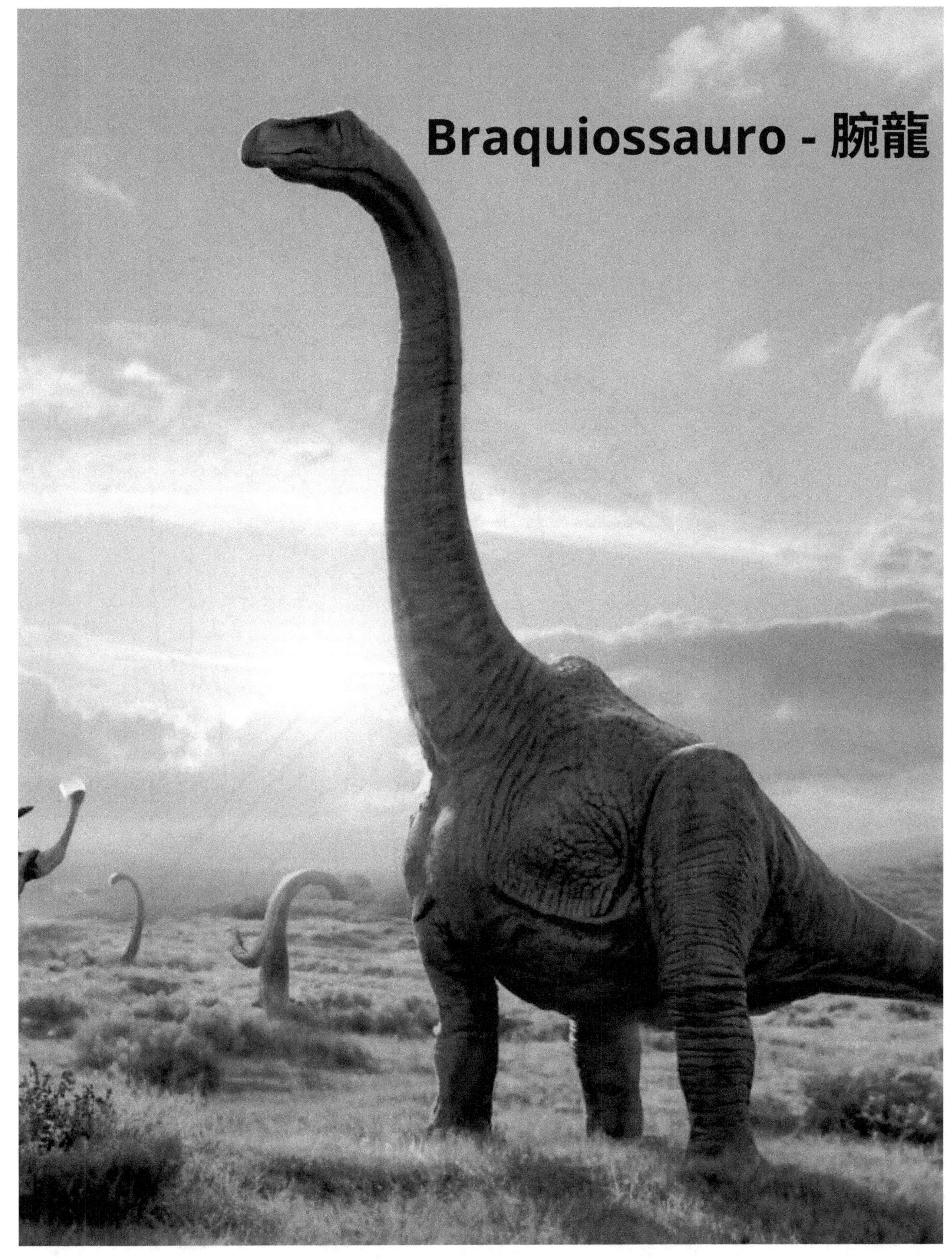
Braquiossauro - 腕龍

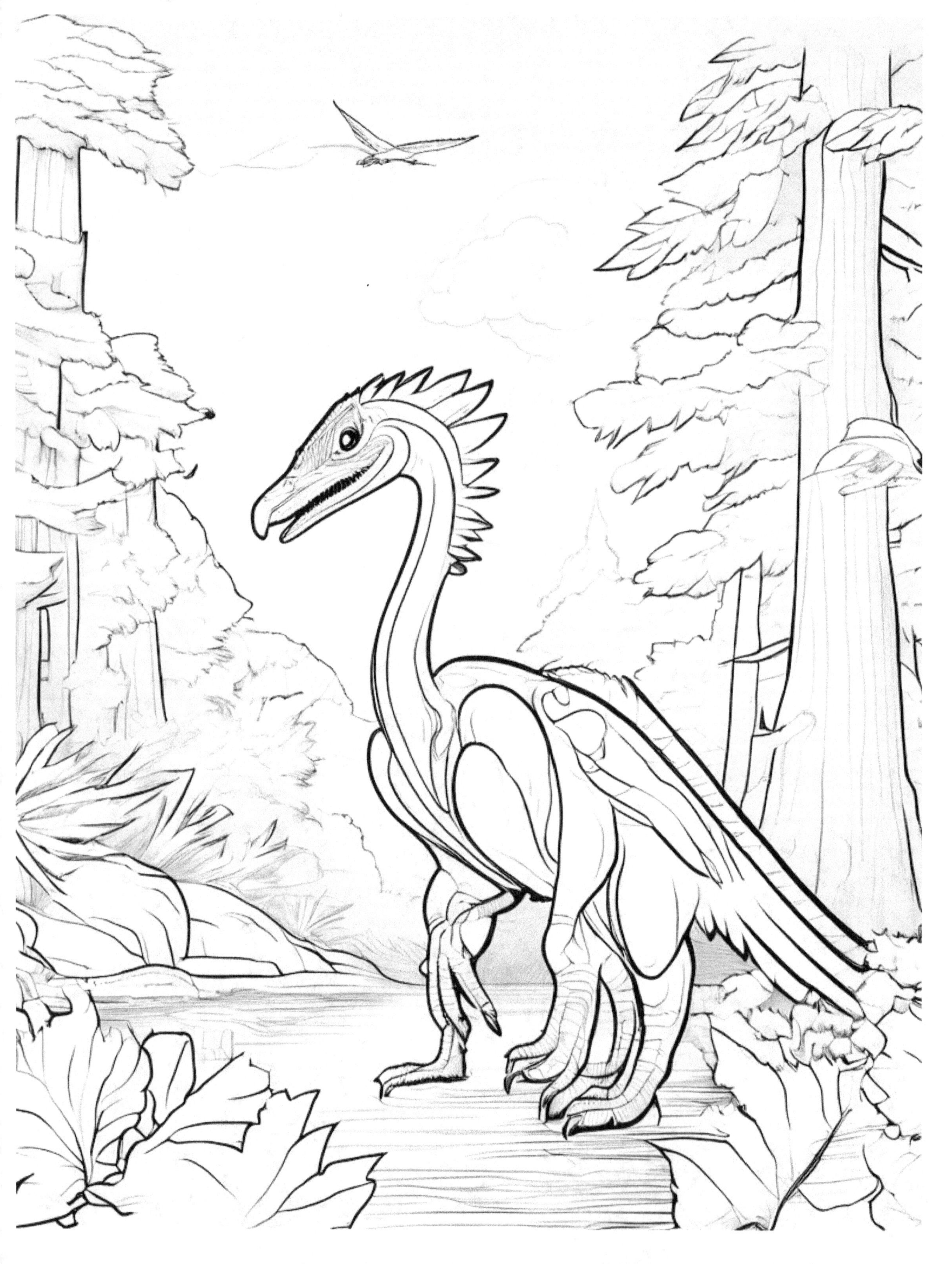

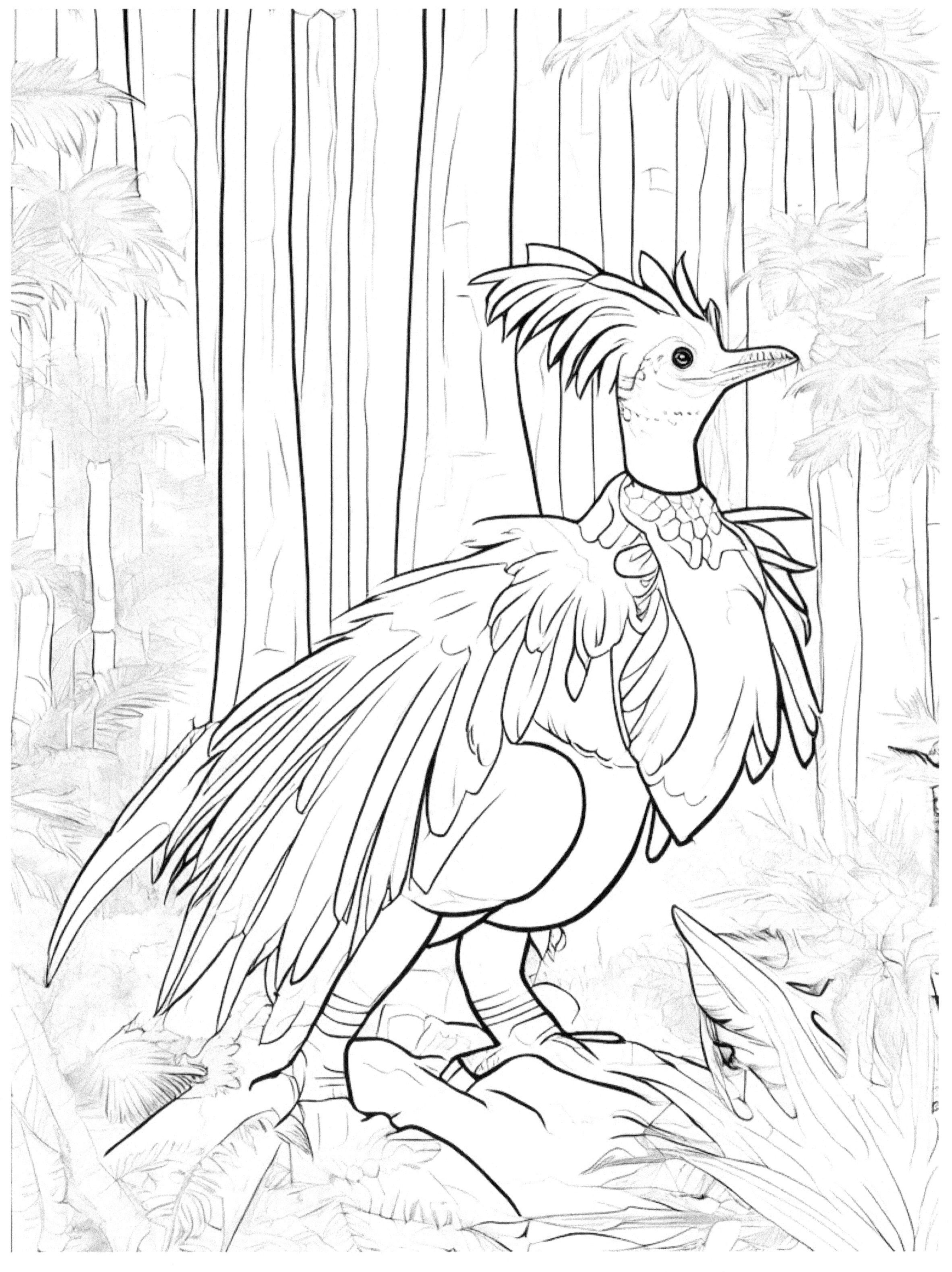

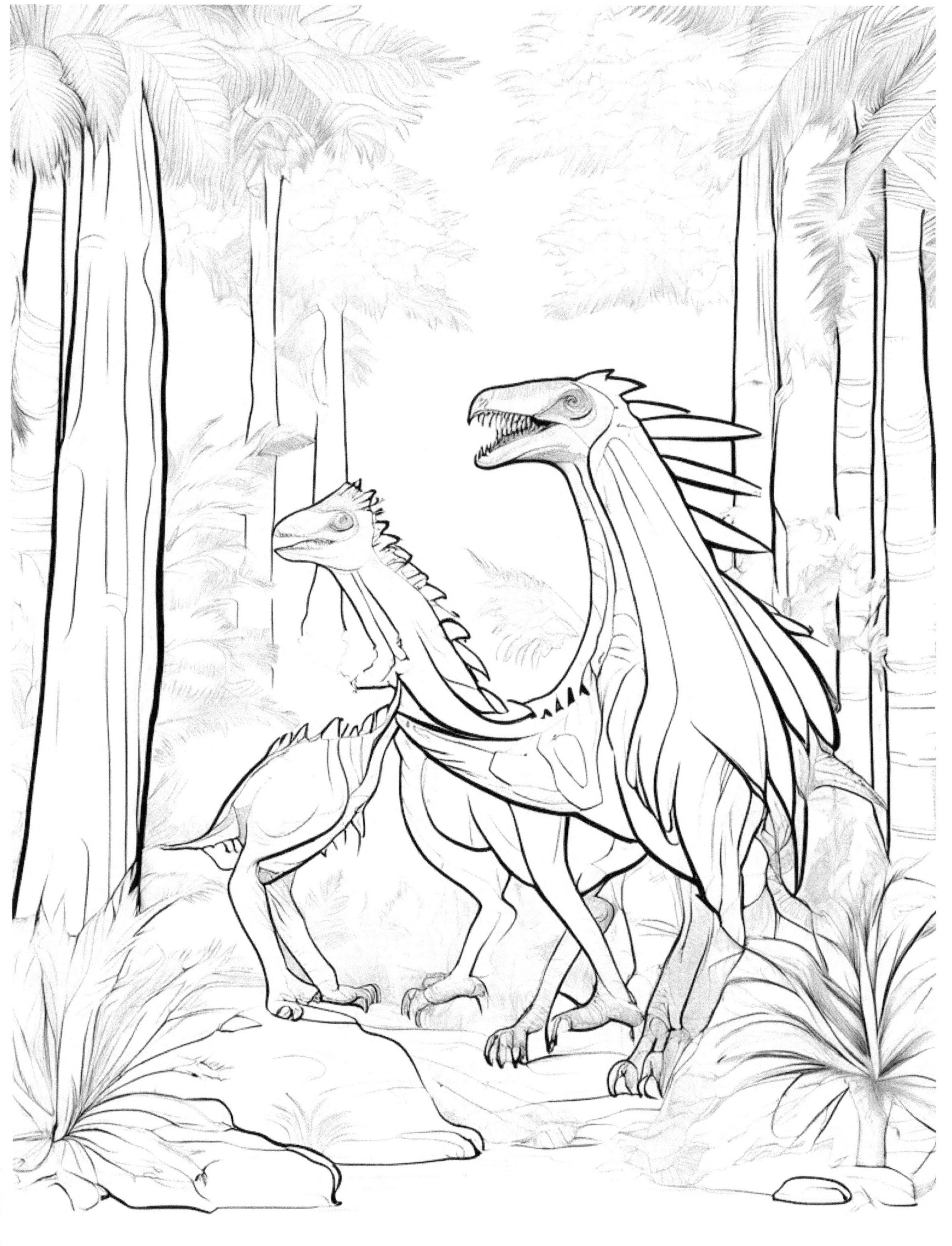

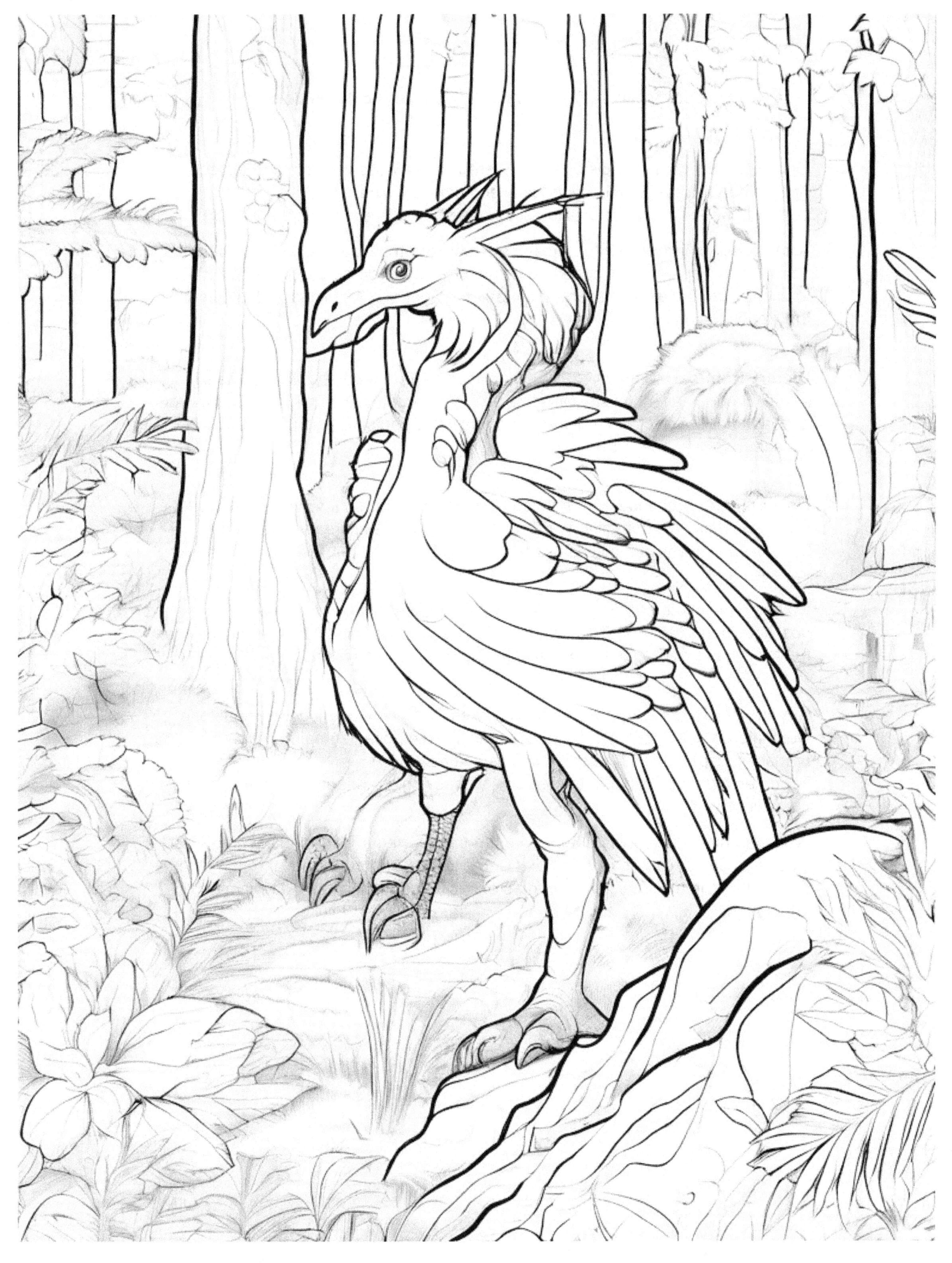

"Archaeopteryx: The Flying Dinosaur of the Jurassic Era"

Once upon a time, in the distant past, there was a dinosaur that defied expectations: Archeopteryx, a fascinating hybrid between dinosaur and bird.
Let's explore the secrets of this incredible being who lived in the Jurassic Era!

Archeopteryx in the Heights: Imagine a dinosaur the size of a common bird, like a crow. Archeopteryx was about the height of an average person, making it closer to us than other giant dinosaurs. With feathers adorning his wings and tail, he was truly a unique sight.

Dietary Habits: Unlike some ferocious dinosaurs, Archeopteryx was primarily insectivorous, feeding on small insects and invertebrates. Their feathers and wings, although not as effective for flight as modern birds, indicate a possible ability to glide from tree to tree in search of food.

How it Lived: Archeopteryx inhabited wooded environments, where its ability to climb trees and its adaptation to partial flight helped it explore its territory. It is believed that it was an agile dinosaur, capable of moving both on the ground and in trees.

Places where it lived: Fossils of Archeopteryx were found in the region that is now known as Germany. This flying dinosaur shared its habitat with other creatures from the Jurassic Era, creating a unique and diverse ecosystem.

Adventures in the Heights: Curious children, imagine exploring the prehistoric world alongside Archeopteryx! Imagine this flying dinosaur jumping between branches, capturing small insects with its unique agility.
Together you could explore the treetops, witnessing the beauty and complexity of Jurassic life.

When learning about Archeopteryx, we are transported to a fascinating time when dinosaurs and birds began to coexist. Come join us on this journey through time, discovering the mysteries and wonders of this unique dinosaur and its incredible adaptations!

Archaeoptery

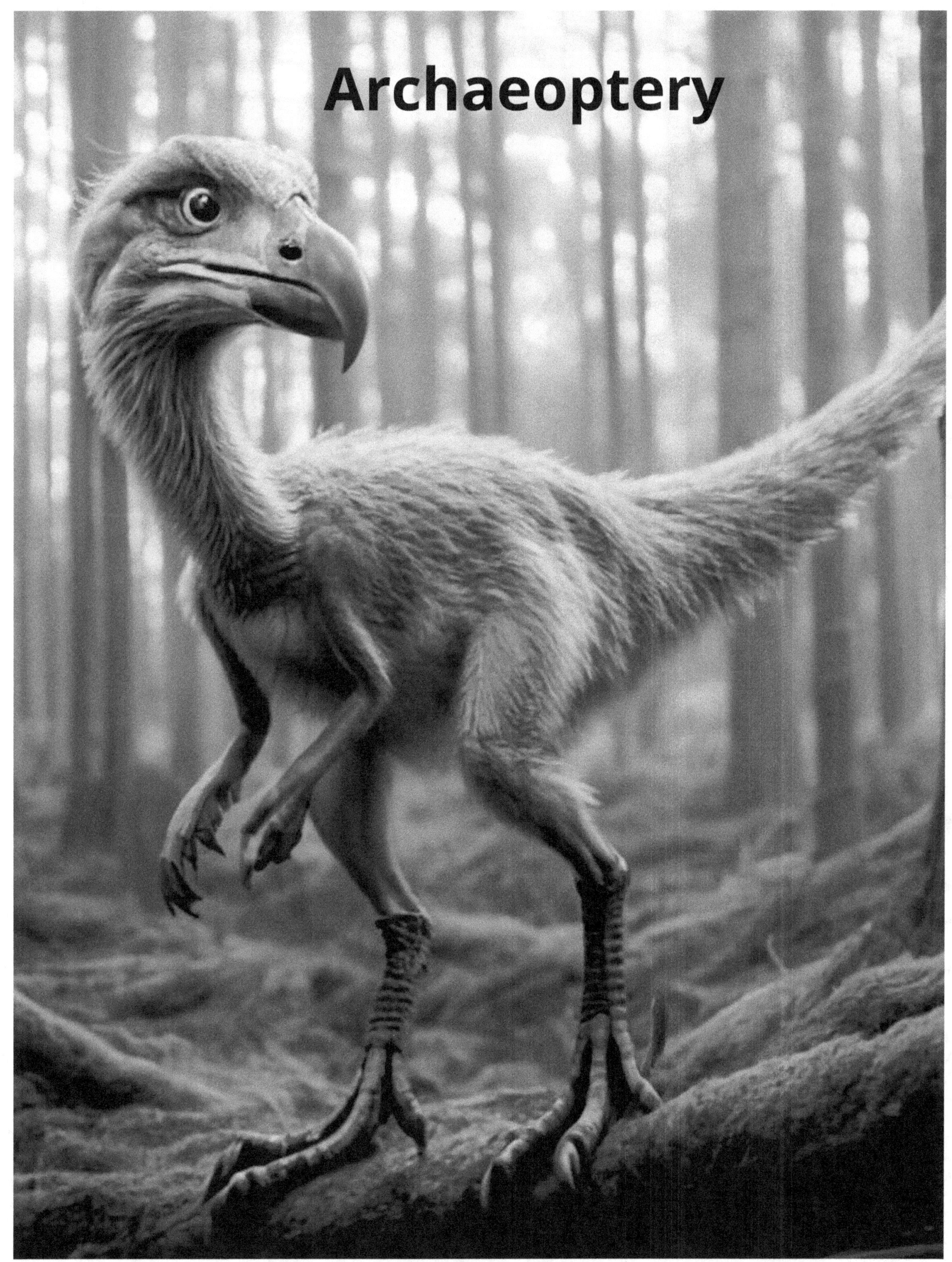

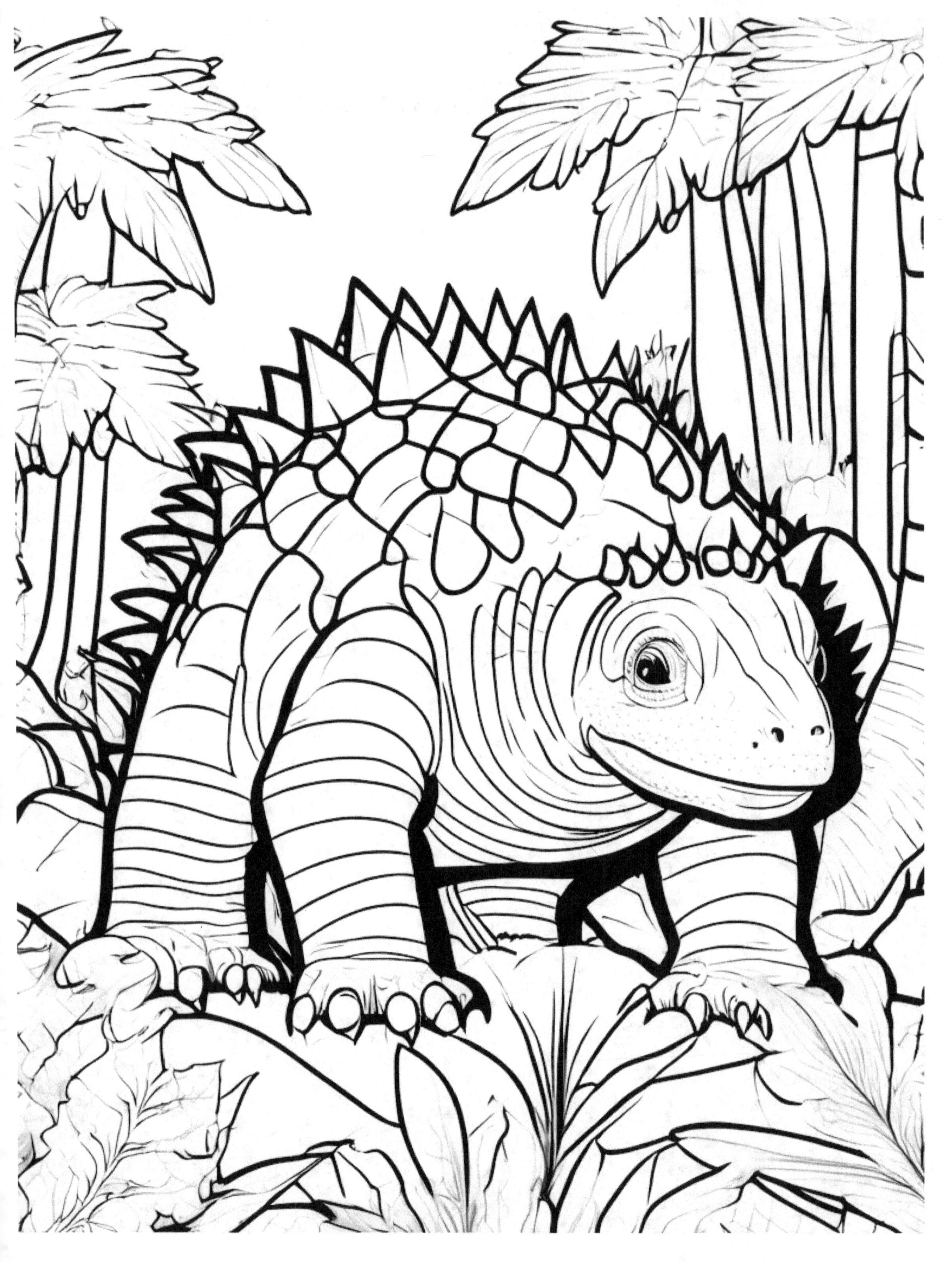

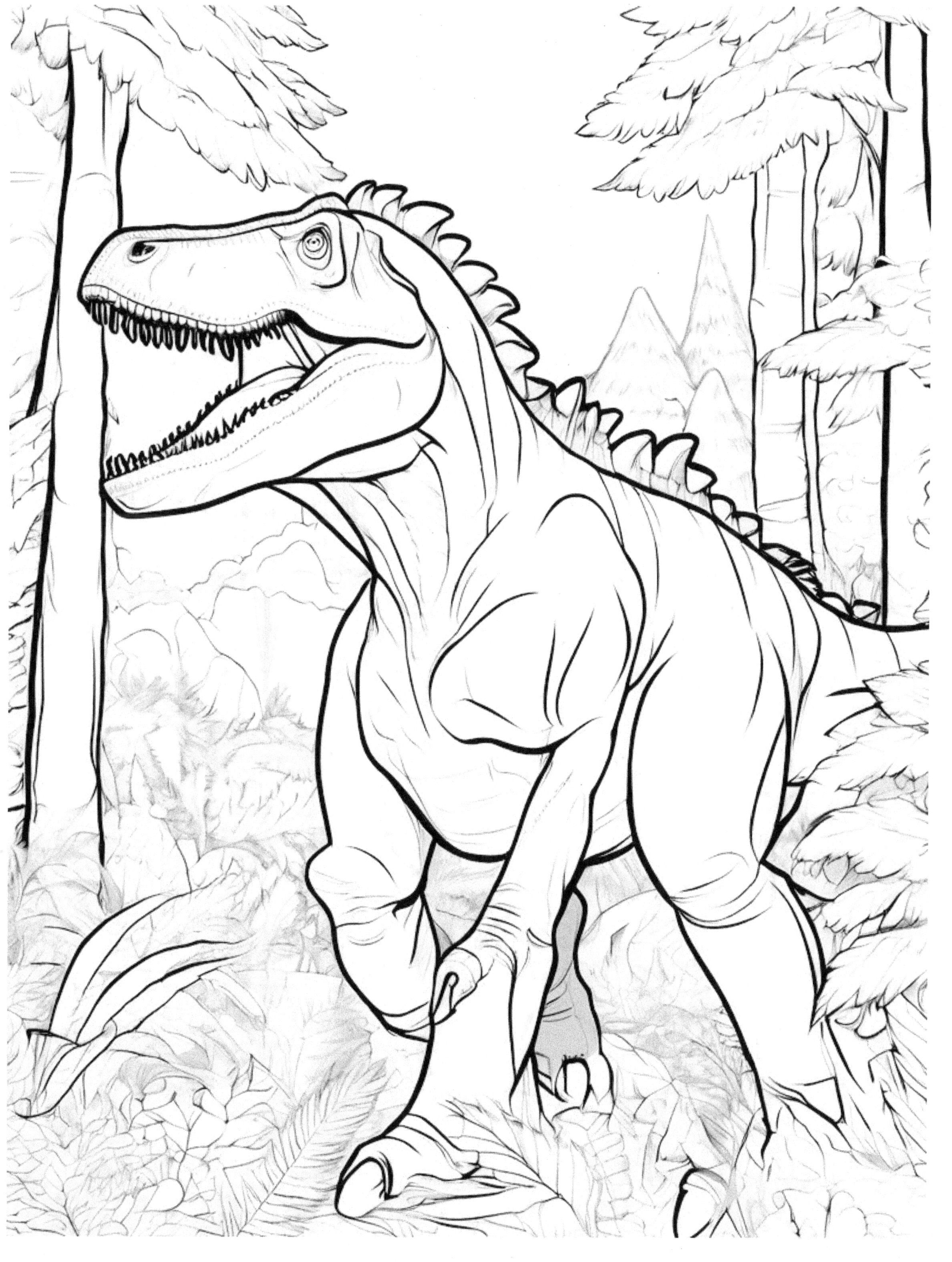

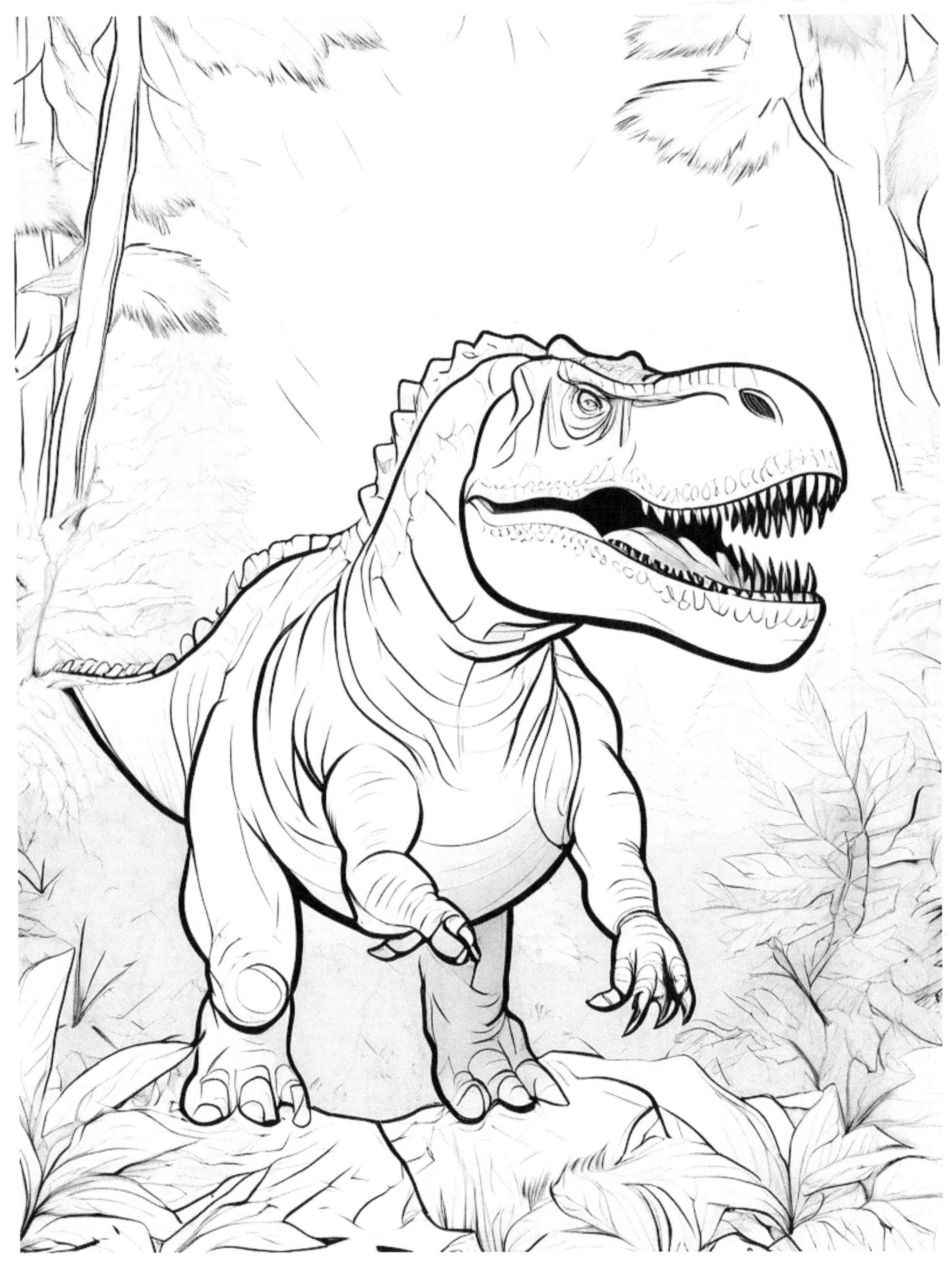

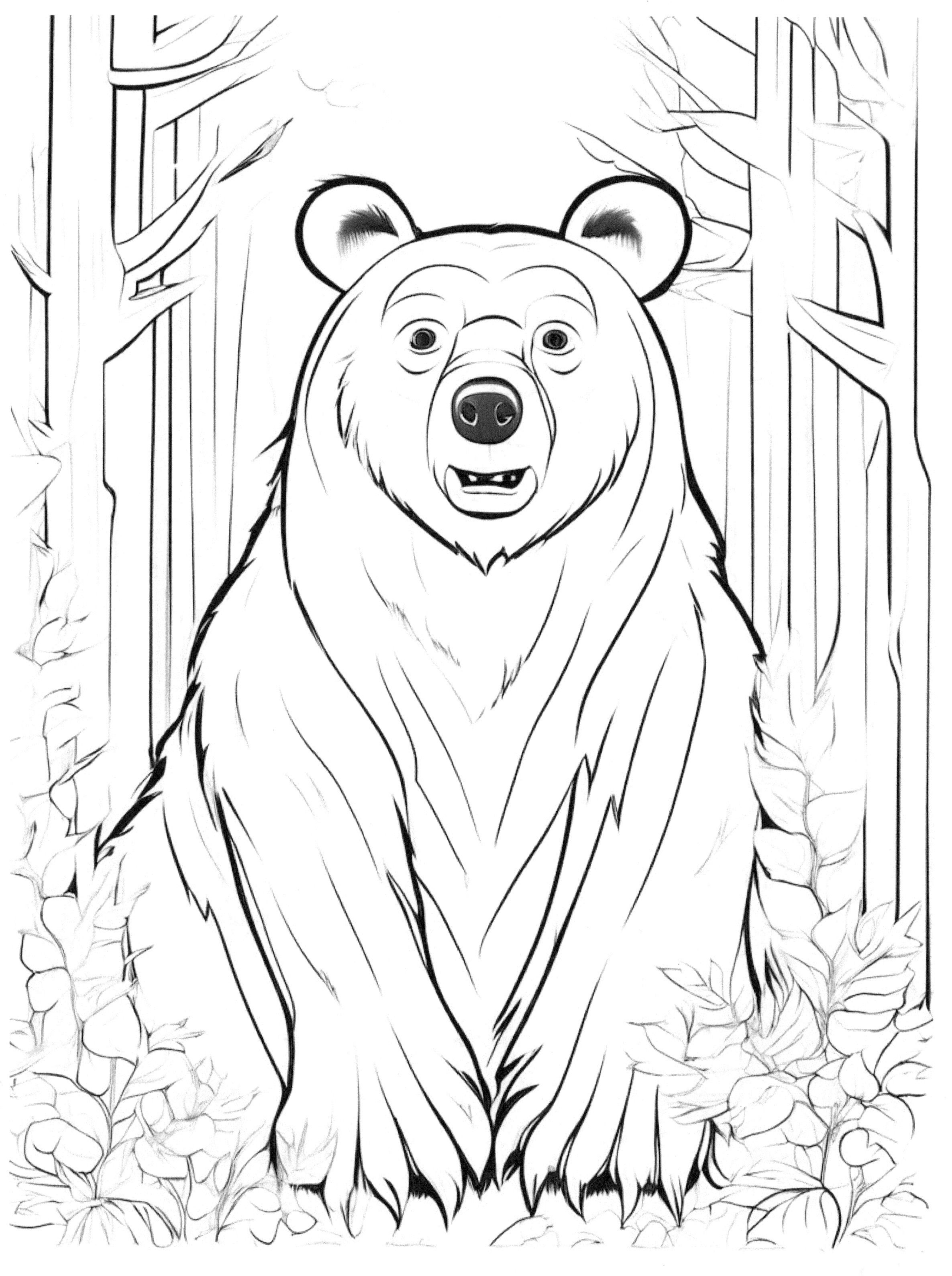

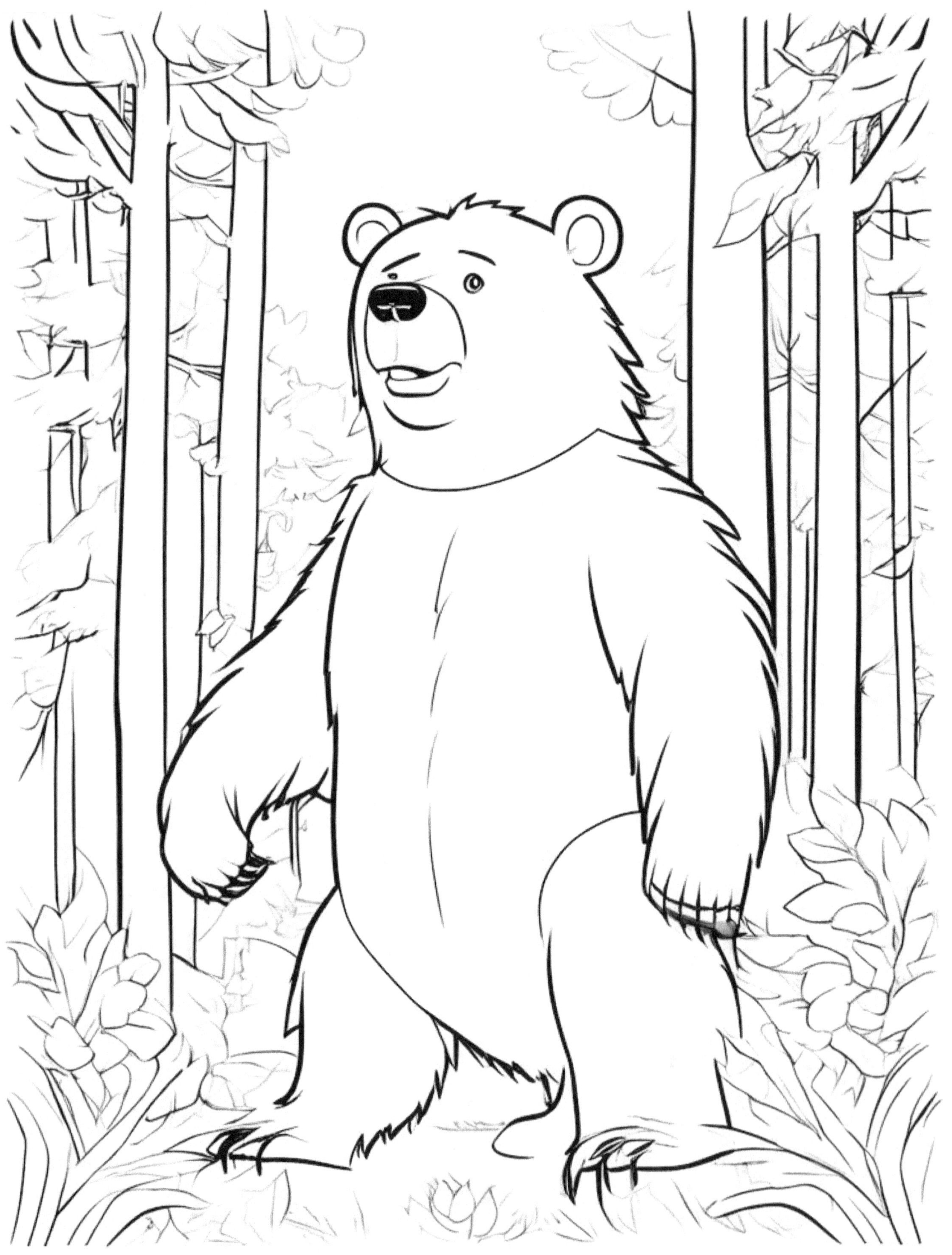